The Quotable

JEFFERSON DAVIS

❧ THE LOCHLAINN SEABROOK COLLECTION ❧

Five-Star Books & Gifts From the Heart of the American South

❧ SeaRavenPress.com ❧

The Quotable
JEFFERSON DAVIS

SELECTIONS FROM THE WRITINGS & SPEECHES OF THE CONFEDERACY'S FIRST PRESIDENT

———•◦❖◦•———

Collected, Edited, & Illustrated, with an Introduction & Notes by Colonel

LOCHLAINN SEABROOK

JEFFERSON DAVIS HISTORICAL GOLD MEDAL WINNER

Foreword by Percival Beacroft, B.A., J.D.

2017

SEA RAVEN PRESS, NASHVILLE, TENNESSEE

THE QUOTABLE JEFFERSON DAVIS

Published by
Sea Raven Press, Cassidy Ravensdale, President
PO Box 1484, Spring Hill, Tennessee 37174-1484 USA
SeaRavenPress.com • searavenpress@gmail.com

Sea Raven Press

Enlightening, educational, & entertaining books for the whole family!

1ˢᵗ SRP paperback edition, 1ˢᵗ printing: August 2011, ISBN: 978-0-9838185-1-9
1ˢᵗ SRP paperback edition, 2ⁿᵈ printing: September 2015, ISBN: 978-0-9838185-1-9
1ˢᵗ SRP hardcover edition, 1ˢᵗ printing: January 2016, ISBN: 978-1-943737-14-7
1ˢᵗ SRP paperback edition, 3ʳᵈ printing: March 2017, ISBN: 978-0-9838185-1-9
1ˢᵗ SRP hardcover edition, 2ⁿᵈ printing: March 2017, ISBN: 978-1-943737-14-7

ISBN: 978-0-9838185-1-9 (paperback)
Library of Congress Control Number: 2011934963

The Quotable Jefferson Davis: Selections from the Writings and Speeches of the
Confederacy's First President, collected and edited, with an introduction and notes,
by Lochlainn Seabrook. Foreword by Percival Beacroft. Includes endnotes and
bibliographical references.

Front and back cover design and art, book design, layout, and interior art by Lochlainn Seabrook.
All images, graphic design, graphic art, and illustrations copyright © Lochlainn Seabrook.
Front cover photo: C.S. President Jefferson Davis

The views on the American "Civil War" documented in this book *are* those of the publisher.

The paper used in this book is acid-free and lignin-free. It has been certified by the Sustainable Forestry
Initiative and the Forest Stewardship Council and meets all ANSI standards for archival quality paper.

PRINTED & MANUFACTURED IN OCCUPIED TENNESSEE, FORMER CONFEDERATE STATES OF AMERICA

Dedication

To the heroic and noble Jefferson Davis, patriot of patriots.

Epigraph

"The underrating of Jefferson Davis
is almost like a giant conspiracy."

Shelby Foote (1916 - 2005)

CONTENTS

TENNESSEE MADE

"Beauvoir House," Biloxi, Mississippi. Located on the Gulf of Mexico on what is now Beach Blvd., this was Davis' last home. Fully restored, Beauvoir is open for public tours and is today owned and operated by the Sons of Confederate Veterans—an organization to which the author proudly belongs.

∾ NOTES TO THE READER ∾

☞ In an effort to retain the true character and meaning of Jefferson Davis' words, they have been printed here exactly as they appear in the original manuscripts, including typographical and grammatical peculiarities inherent to 19th-Century Southern writing and speaking.

☞ Davis' quotes are preceded by a traditional Victorian hand pointer. My comments appear in italics above his quotes, while my clarifications are enclosed in brackets within his quotes.

☞ In any study of America's antebellum, bellum, and postbellum periods, it is vitally important to understand that in 1860 the two major political parties—the Democrats and the newly formed Republicans—were the opposite of what they are today. In other words, the Democrats of the mid 19th Century were Conservatives, akin to the Republican Party of today, while the Republicans of the mid 19th Century were Liberals, akin to the Democratic Party of today.

Thus the Confederacy's Democratic president, Jefferson Davis, was a Conservative (with libertarian leanings); the Union's Republican president, Abraham Lincoln, was a Liberal (with socialistic leanings). This is why, in the mid 1800s, the conservative wing of the Democratic Party was known as "the States' Rights Party."[1]

Hence, the Democrats of the Civil War period referred to themselves as "conservatives," "confederates," "anti-centralists," or "constitutionalists" (the latter because they favored strict adherence to the original Constitution—which tacitly guaranteed states' rights—as created by the Founding Fathers), while the Republicans called themselves "liberals," "nationalists," "centralists," or "consolidationists" (the latter three because they wanted to nationalize the central government and consolidate political power in Washington, D.C.).[2]

The author's cousin, Confederate Vice President and Democrat Alexander H. Stephens: a Southern Conservative.

Since this idea is new to most of my readers, let us further demystify it by viewing it from the perspective of the American Revolutionary War. If Davis and his conservative Southern constituents (the Democrats of 1861) had been alive in 1775, they would have sided with George Washington and the American colonists, who sought to secede from the tyrannical government of Great Britain; if Lincoln and his Liberal Northern constituents (the Republicans of 1861) had been alive at that time, they would have sided with King George III and the English monarchy, who sought to maintain the American colonies as possessions of the British Empire. It is due to this very comparison that Southerners often refer to the "Civil War" as the Second American Revolutionary War.[3]

☞ As I heartily dislike the phrase "Civil War," its use throughout this book (as well as in my other works) is worthy of an explanation.

Today America's entire literary system refers to the conflict of 1861 using the Northern term the "Civil War," whether we in the South like it or not. Thus, as all book searches by readers, libraries, and retail outlets are now performed online, and as all bookstores categorize works from this period under the heading "Civil War," book publishers and authors who deal with this particular topic have little choice but to use this term themselves. If I were to refuse to use it, as some of my Southern colleagues have suggested, few people would ever find or read my books.

Add to this the fact that scarcely any non-Southerners have ever heard of the names we in the South use for the conflict, such as the "War for Southern Independence"—or my personal preference, "Lincoln's War." It only makes sense then to use the term "Civil War" in most commercial situations.

We should also bear in mind that while today educated persons, particularly educated Southerners, all share an abhorrence for the phrase "Civil War," it was not always so. Confederates who lived through and even fought in the conflict regularly used the term throughout the 1860s, and even long after. Among them were Confederate generals such as Nathan Bedford Forrest, Richard Taylor, and Joseph E. Johnston, not to mention the Confederacy's vice president, Alexander H. Stephens.

In 1895 my cousin General James Longstreet wrote about his military experiences in a work subtitled, *Memoirs of the Civil War in America*. Even the Confederacy's highest leader, President Jefferson Davis, used the term "Civil War,"[4] and in one case at least, as late as 1881—the year he wrote his brilliant exposition, *The Rise and Fall of the Confederate Government*.[5]

☞ Neither slavery or Lincoln's War on the American people and the Constitution can ever be fully understood without a thorough knowledge of the South's perspective. As *The Quotable Jefferson Davis* is only meant to be a brief introductory guide to these topics, one cannot hope to learn the whole truth about them here. For those who are interested in a more in-depth study, please see my other more scholarly books, listed on page 2; in particular, my title, *Everything You Were Taught About the Civil War is Wrong, Ask a Southerner!*

THE NORTH IS STILL LYING ABOUT LINCOLN'S WAR

"When, in after times, the passions of the day shall have subsided, and all the evidence shall have been collected and compared, the philosophical inquirer, who asks why the majority of the stronger section invaded the peaceful homes of their late associates, will be answered by History: 'The lust of empire impelled them to wage against their weaker neighbors a war of subjugation.'"[6]

Jefferson Davis

FOREWORD

Little did Jefferson Davis, the first President of the new country to be known as "The Confederate States of America," know that his position as chief executive was to be far more difficult than that of Washington. He was to lead a country without a currency or treasury, without a military force, and without munitions, create a government, and almost immediately face an invading enemy with five times the manpower, and an army and navy that he himself had modernized only a few years before as U.S. Secretary of War. He kept the enemy at bay for four years and came close to winning. His governmental career had been a great foundation for his leadership. He was a former Congressman, a Senator from Mississippi, and Secretary of War under Franklin Pierce. If not for the War in 1861, he would probably have been President of the United States.

Davis struggled against innumerable obstacles, and he was much the same as a Churchill in his determination to avoid surrender at all costs. He was a well educated statesman and a graduate of West Point. He was reared in a deep belief in the Constitution and his constitutional principles led him to accept the presidency out of a devotion to duty—a duty to his former country, the United States of America, and now to the Confederate States of America. The Confederate Constitution was, in the main, the U.S. Constitution with minor changes, such as giving the States the right to decide upon the slavery issue. Unknown to most, slavery was protected in the U.S. Constitution in 1861, but the South felt that this was an issue for the States to decide, and thus this provision was included in the new C.S. Constitution.

Helping to preserve Davis' memory is prolific historian and author Colonel Lochlainn Seabrook, a cousin of the president's first wife Sarah Knox Taylor. In his unique and absorbing book, *The Quotable Jefferson Davis*, we get a glimpse into the many thoughts, beliefs, and policies of Davis. Clearly presented, Seabrook's selections capture the brilliance, education, and vision of this noble American figure. Excerpts from his many speeches as well as from his book, *The Rise and Fall of the Confederate Government*, reveal, as never before, why Davis was selected to be the Confederacy's first chief executive.

As a Trustee of the Papers of Jefferson Davis since 1973 and one of the founders of the Davis Family Association, I cannot recommend this book highly enough. It is a must-read for anyone interested in the real Jefferson Davis, as opposed to the false one so often presented in mainstream history books.

Percival Beacroft, B.A., J.D.
Houston, Texas
March 2017

∽ INTRODUCTION ∽

Abraham Lincoln was, by and large, a poor writer and a mediocre speechmaker whose only known literary effort was an atheistic book devoted to his lifelong views that the Bible is an outrageous fiction filled with fairy tales, there is no such thing as a miracle, Jesus was a "bastard," and those who call themselves Christians are "ignoramuses." Fortunately for irreligious Lincoln, though unfortunately for us, his employer at the time threw this remarkable book into the fire in order to save his employee's future reputation.[7]

Despite the sixteenth president's overt lack of formal education, linguistic abilities, and writing talent, or even the penning of his "little book" condemning God and Christianity, innumerable works of his quotes have been lovingly published, many with statements that Lincoln never even made.

Jefferson Davis at age thirty-two, just prior to becoming a member of the U.S. House of Representatives.

Contrast Bible-loathing anti-Christian Lincoln with the Southern Confederacy's first president: Bible-believing Christian Jefferson Davis. Davis was a brilliant thinker, orator, speech writer, and author who penned several outstanding scholarly books that have rightly become classics, particularly here in the South. And yet no one has thought to dedicate a single volume to his many impressive, sophisticated, astute, commonsensical, and inspirational quotes.

Ostensibly, Lincoln is quoted and Davis is not because the former won the War for the Southern Independence (still incorrectly called the "Civil War" by Northerners) while the latter lost. Being of Southern descent, Confederate blood, and a relation of President Davis, I felt this was a situation that needed correcting. The book you now hold in your hand is the result.

Having spent many years studying Lincoln's words and having written numerous books on the liberal chief executive, I have come to know the man and his manner of thinking quite well. Having researched conservative Davis' writings for nearly as long, I am struck by the extreme differences between the two men, not only politically of course, but particularly in the arena of language.

Where Lincoln is confusing and obscure, Davis is clear and accessible. Where Lincoln is uninformed (especially in regards to American history and the U.S. Constitution), Davis is overtly knowledgeable. Where Lincoln is purposefully nefarious and obfuscatory, Davis is direct and open. Where Lincoln is tedious, unimaginative, and rhetorical, Davis is concise, ingenious, and improvisational.

Where Lincoln is derivative, Davis is original. Where Lincoln is misleading and duplicitous, Davis is candid and honest. Where Lincoln seems to be running the U.S. according to his personal ideologies and political aspirations, Davis runs the Confederacy impartially and in strict accordance with the Constitution. Where Lincoln is a conformist (as Illinois Senator Stephen A. Douglas and others often pointed out), Davis is an individual. The list is endless.

Anyone who *thoroughly* and *objectively* examines the words of both men will inevitably come to the same conclusions. In short, there could not have been two more dissimilar individuals leading the Confederacy and the Union during those dark days between 1861 and 1865.

Lincoln has now had more than his say, and hundreds of books a year continue to be admiringly written about "Honest Abe," nearly all of them brimming with falsehoods, disinformation, and anti-South propaganda, particularly in regards to Davis and the War. How predictable and tiresome.

Davis: Kentuckian, West Point graduate, Mexican-American War veteran, U.S. Senator, Mississippi Representative, U.S. Secretary of War, and C.S. President.

It is now time to hear President Jefferson Davis' side of the story. In his elegant mannerisms, fresh open-faced speech, fiery and exciting phraseology, and clear elevated writings, we find the essence of the American Revolution, the heart and soul of the Founding Fathers, and the promise of an America that will one day return to its authentic constitutional roots: states' rights.

In Davis we have a true American patriot, a man whose every molecule was made up of the very rugged individualism and freedom-loving spirit that gave birth to this great Confederate Republic of ours in 1781.

Let us now hear the highly revered Southern chief executive speak. Hear Jefferson Davis prove that Lincoln's war on the South was not only unholy, but also unconstitutional, illegal, and far from "irrepressible." Let his words ring out like the Liberty Bell. Let a whole new generation be inspired.

Lochlainn Seabrook
Franklin, Tennessee, USA
August 2011

"Nothing fills me with deeper sadness than to see a Southern man apologizing for the defense we made of our inheritance. Our cause was so just, so sacred, that had I known all that has come to pass, had I known what was to be inflicted upon me, all that my country has suffered, all that our posterity was to endure, I would do it all over again."

Jefferson Davis, 1881

The Quotable

JEFFERSON DAVIS

1

GOVERNMENT

☛ "[It is clear that the Founding Fathers] did not mean to give any countenance to the idea which . . . has again reared its mischievous crest in these latter days—that the government which they organized was a consolidated nationality, instead of a confederacy of sovereign members."[8]

Davis Family at their home "Beauvoir," near Biloxi, Mississippi, in 1884 or 1885. Left to right: the President's granddaughter Varina Howell Davis Hayes (1878-1934), his daughter Margaret Howell Davis (1855-1909), his granddaughter Lucy White Hayes (1882-1966), and President Davis.

☛ " . . . in the very front of their Articles of Confederation, they [the Founding Fathers] set forth the conspicuous declaration that each State retained 'its sovereignty, freedom, and independence.'"[9]

☛ "Our Government is an agency of delegated and strictly limited powers. Its founders did not look to its preservation by force; but the chain they wove to bind these States together was one of love and mutual good offices. They had broken the fetters of despotic power; they had separated themselves from the mother-country [Britain] upon the question of community independence; and their sons will be degenerate indeed if, clinging to the mere name and forms of free government, they forge and rivet upon their posterity the fetters which their ancestors broke."[10]

☞ "[According to the principle of American republicanism] . . . the people never do transfer their right of sovereignty, either in whole or in part. They only delegate to their governments the exercise of such of its functions as may be necessary, subject always to their own control, and to reassumption whenever such government fails to fulfill the purposes for which it was instituted."[11]

☞ "Mr. [James] Madison, one of the most distinguished of the men of that day and of the advocates of the Constitution, in a speech . . . in the Virginia Convention of 1788, explained that 'We, the people,' who were to establish the Constitution, were the people of 'thirteen Sovereignties.'

"In the *Federalist*, he repeatedly employs the term—as, for example, when he says: 'Do they (the fundamental principles of the Confederation) require that, in the establishment of the Constitution, the States should be regarded as distinct and independent Sovereigns? They are so regarded by the Constitution proposed.'"[12]

To big government Liberals concerning the term 'state sovereignty':
☞ "[They seem] unable even to comprehend that it means the sovereignty, not of State governments, but of people who make them. With minds preoccupied by the unreal idea of one great people of a consolidated nation, these gentlemen are blinded to the plain and primary truth that the only way in which the people ordained the Constitution was as the people of States."[13]

☞ "If any lingering doubt could have existed as to the reservation of their entire sovereignty by the people of the respective States, when they organized the Federal Union, it would have been removed by the adoption of the tenth amendment to the Constitution, which was not only one of the amendments proposed by various States when ratifying that instrument, but the particular one in which they substantially agreed, and upon which they most urgently insisted. Indeed, it is quite certain that the Constitution would never have received the assent and ratification of Massachusetts, New Hampshire, New York, North Carolina, and perhaps other States, but for a well-grounded assurance that the substance of this amendment would be adopted as soon as the requisite formalities could be complied with. That amendment is in these words: 'The powers not delegated to the United States by the Constitution nor prohibited by it to the States are reserved to the States respectively, or to the people.'"[14]

☞ "Our present political position has been achieved in a manner unprecedented in the history of nations. It illustrates the American idea that governments rest on the consent of the governed, and that it is the right of the people to alter or abolish them whenever they become destructive of the ends for which they were established."[15]

☞ "When certain sovereign and independent States form a union with limited powers for some general purposes, and any one or more of them, in the progress of time, suffer unjust and oppressive grievances for which there is no redress but in a withdrawal from the association, is such withdrawal an insurrection? If so, then of what advantage is a compact of union to States? Within the Union are oppressions and grievances; and the attempt to go out brings war and subjugation. The ambitious and aggressive States obtain possession of the central authority which, having grown strong in the lapse of time, asserts its entire sovereignty over the States. Whichever of them denies it and seeks to retire, is declared to be guilty of insurrection, its citizens are stigmatized as 'rebels,' as if they had revolted against a master, and a war of subjugation is begun. If this action is once tolerated, where will it end? Where is the value of constitutional liberty? What strength is there in bills of rights—in limitations of power?"[16]

☞ "[In the late 1700s] Massachusetts and New Hampshire, in their ordinances of ratification [of the U.S. Constitution], expressing the opinion 'that certain amendments and alterations in the said Constitution would remove the fears and quiet the apprehensions of many of the good people of this Commonwealth, and more effectually guard against an undue administration of the Federal Government,' each recommended several such amendments, putting this at the head in the following form: 'That it be explicitly declared that all powers not expressly delegated by the aforesaid Constitution are reserved to the several States, to be by them exercised.' Of course, those stanch [that is, staunch] republican communities meant the people of the States—not their governments, as something distinct from their people."[17]

☞ "[Before ratifying the U.S. Constitution, the state of] New York expressed herself as follows: 'That the powers of government may be reassumed by the people whenever it shall become necessary to their happiness; that every power, jurisdiction, and right, which is not by the said Constitution clearly delegated to the Congress of the United States, or the departments of the Government thereof, remains to the people of the several States, or to their respective State governments, to whom they may have granted the same; and that those clauses in the said Constitution, which declare that Congress shall not have or exercise certain powers, do not imply that Congress is entitled to any powers not given by the said Constitution; but such clauses are to be construed either as exceptions to certain specified powers or as inserted merely for greater caution.'"[18]

☛ "[Before ratifying the U.S. Constitution, the state of] South Carolina expressed the idea thus: 'This Convention doth also declare that no section or paragraph of the said Constitution warrants a construction that the States do not retain every power not expressly relinquished by them and vested in the General Government of the Union.'"[19]

☛ "[Before ratifying the U.S. Constitution, the state of] North Carolina proposed it in these terms: 'Each State in the Union shall respectively retain every power, jurisdiction, and right, which is not by this Constitution delegated to the Congress of the United States or to the departments of the General Government.'"[20]

☛ "Rhode Island gave in her long-withheld assent to the Constitution, 'in full confidence' that certain proposed amendments would be adopted, the first of which was expressed in these words: 'That Congress shall guarantee to each State its Sovereignty, freedom, and independence, and every power, jurisdiction, and right, which is not by this Constitution expressly delegated to the United States.'

"This was in May, 1790, when nearly three years had been given to discussion and explanation of the new Government by its founders and others, when it had been in actual operation for more than a year, and when there was every advantage for a clear understanding of its nature and principles. Under such circumstances, and in the 'full confidence' that this language expressed its meaning and intent, the people of Rhode Island signified their 'accession' to the 'Confederate Republic' of the States already united.

"No objection was made from any quarter to the principle asserted in these various forms, or to the amendment in which it was finally expressed, although many thought it unnecessary, as being merely declaratory of what would have been sufficiently obvious without it—that the functions of the Government of the United States were strictly limited to the exercise of such powers as were expressly delegated, and that the people of the several States retained all others.

"Is it compatible with reason to suppose that people so chary of the delegation of specific powers or functions could have meant to surrender or transfer the very basis and origin of all power—their inherent sovereignty—and this, not by express grant, but by implication?"[21]

☛ "If the [tyrannical] doctrines thus announced by the Government of the United States are conceded, then, look through either end of the political telescope, and one sees only an empire, and the once famous Declaration of Independence trodden in the dust as a 'glittering generality,' and the compact of union denounced as a 'flaunting lie.' Those who submit to such consequences without resistance are not worthy of the liberties and the rights to which they were born, and deserve to be made slaves. Such must be the verdict of mankind."[22]

☛ "Blood, much and precious, was expended to vindicate and to establish community independence, and the great American idea that all governments rest on the consent of the governed, and that the people may at their will alter or abolish their government, however or by whomsoever instituted."[23]

☛ ". . . in this country, the only political community—the only independent corporate unit—through which the people can exercise their sovereignty, is the State. Minor communities—as those of counties, cities, and towns—are merely fractional subdivisions of the State; and these do not affect the evidence that there was not such a political community as the 'people of the United States in the aggregate.'"[24]

☛ "That the States were severally sovereign and independent when they were united under the Articles of Confederation, is distinctly asserted in those articles, and is admitted even by the extreme partisans of consolidation [that is, in modern parlance, big government Liberals]. Of right, they [the states] are still sovereign, unless they have surrendered or been divested of their sovereignty; and those who deny the proposition have been vainly called upon to point out the process by which they have divested themselves, or have been divested of it, otherwise than by usurpation."[25]

☛ "The illustrious [George] Washington, who presided over the Philadelphia Convention [in 1787], in his correspondence, repeatedly refers to the proposed Union as a 'Confederacy' of States, or a 'confederated Government,' and to the several States as 'acceding,' or signifying their 'accession,' to it, in ratifying the Constitution. He refers to the Constitution itself as 'a compact or treaty,' and classifies it among compacts or treaties between 'men, bodies of men, or countries.'"[26]

☛ "Our fathers, learning wisdom from the experiments of Rome and of Greece—the one a consolidated republic, and the other strictly a confederacy—and taught by the lessons of our own experiment under the [U.S.] Confederation [1781 to 1789], came together to form a Constitution for 'a more perfect union,' and, in my judgment, made the best government which has ever been instituted by man. It only requires that it should be carried out in the spirit in which it was made, that the circumstances under which it was made should continue, and no evil can arise under this Government for which it has not an appropriate remedy. Then it is outside of the Government—elsewhere than to its Constitution or to its administration—that we are to look. Men must not creep in the dust of partisan strife and seek to make points against opponents as the means of evading or meeting the issues before us. The fault is not in the form of the Government, nor does the evil spring from the manner in which it has been administered. Where, then, is it? It is that our fathers formed a Government for a Union of friendly States; and though under it the people have been prosperous beyond comparison with any other whose career is recorded in the history of man, still that Union of friendly States has changed its character, and sectional hostility has been substituted for the fraternity in which the Government was founded."[27]

☛ "Now, if there be any one great principle pervading the Federal Constitution, the State Constitutions, the writings of the fathers, the whole American system, as clearly as the sunlight pervades the solar system, it is that no government is sovereign—that all governments derive their powers from the people, and exercise them in subjection to the will of the people—not a will expressed in any irregular, lawless, tumultuary manner, but the will of the organized political community, expressed through authorized and legitimate channels. The founders of the American republics never conferred, nor intended to confer, sovereignty upon either their State or Federal Governments."[28]

☛ "If, then, the people of the States, in forming a Federal Union, surrendered—or . . . transferred—or if they meant to surrender or transfer—part of their sovereignty, to whom was the transfer made? Not to 'the people of the United States in the aggregate'; for there was no such people in existence, and they did not create or constitute such a people by merger of themselves. Not to the Federal Government; for they disclaimed, as a fundamental principle, the sovereignty of any government. There was no such surrender, no such transfer, in whole or in part, expressed or implied. They retained, and intended to retain, their sovereignty in its integrity—undivided and indivisible."[29]

☛ "Civil war there cannot be between States held together by their volition only. This rule of voluntary association, which cannot fail to be conservative, by securing just and impartial government at home, does not diminish the security of the obligations by which the Confederate States may be bound to foreign nations. In proof of this it is to be remembered that, at the first moment of asserting their right of secession, these [Southern] States proposed a settlement on the basis of a common liability for the obligations of the General [U.S.] Government."[30]

On the preposterous belief of Lincoln and other Liberals that the people of the separate states surrendered their sovereignty to the central government upon attaining statehood:
☛ "Clearly not, in accordance with the ideas and principles of those who made the Declaration of Independence, adopted the Articles of Confederation, and established the Constitution of the United States; for in each and all of these the corner-stone is the inherent and inalienable sovereignty of the people. To have transferred sovereignty from the people to a Government would have been to have fought the battles of the [American] Revolution in vain—not for the freedom and independence of the States, but for a mere change of masters. Such a thought or purpose could not have been in the heads or hearts of those who molded the Union, and could have found lodgment only when the ebbing tide of patriotism and fraternity had swept away the landmarks which they erected who sought by the compact of union to secure and perpetuate the liberties then possessed. The men who had won at great cost the independence of their respective States were deeply impressed with the value of union, but they could never have consented, like 'the base Judean,' to fling away the priceless pearl of State sovereignty for any possible alliance."[31]

On the U.S. government before *Southern secession:*

☞ ". . . we are rapidly drifting into a position in which this is to become a government of the army and navy; in which the authority of the United States is to be maintained, not by law, not by constitutional agreement between the States, but by physical force; and will you stand still and see this policy consummated? Will you fold your arms, the degenerate descendants of those men who proclaimed the eternal principle that government rests on the consent of the governed; and that every people have a right to change, modify, or abolish a government when it ceases to answer the ends for which it was established, and permit this Government imperceptibly to slide from the moorings where it was originally anchored, and become a military despotism? [This is] not the Government instituted by our fathers; and against it, so long as I live, with heart and hand, I will rebel."[32]

On the U.S. government after *Southern secession:*

☞ "The experiment instituted by our Revolutionary fathers, of a voluntary union of sovereign States for purposes specified in a solemn compact, had been perverted by those who, feeling power and forgetting right, were determined to respect no law but their own will. The Government had ceased to answer the ends for which it was ordained and established. To save ourselves from a revolution which, in its silent but rapid progress, was about to place us under the despotism of numbers, and to preserve in spirit, as well as in form, a system of government we believed to be peculiarly fitted to our condition, and full of promise for mankind, we determined to make a new association, composed of States homogenous in interest, in policy and in feeling."[33]

2

CONSTITUTIONAL

PRINCIPLES

Southern icon President Davis in the late 1880s.

☛ ". . . the [U.S.] Constitution, . . . a bundle of compromises, . . . is the life-blood of the Union."[34]

☛ "[The] principle of State sovereignty and independence . . . was regarded by the fathers of the Union as the corner-stone of the structure and the basis of the hope for its perpetuity."[35]

☛ "Each of the states was originally declared to be sovereign and independent."[36]

☛ "If the Government is the result of a union of States, then these States must be separate, sovereign, and distinct, to be able to form a union, which is entirely an act of their own volition."[37]

On Lincoln's flagrant disregard and even contempt for the U.S. Constitution:
☛ "The commands of the Constitution are positive, direct, unchanged, and unrelaxed by circumstances. They are equally in force in a state of war and in a state of peace. The powers are delegated, and can not be amended or changed by war or peace. Its words are these: 'This Constitution, and the laws of the United States, which shall be made in pursuance thereof, shall be

the supreme law, and the judges in every State shall be bound thereby, anything in the Constitution or laws of any State to the contrary notwithstanding. The Senators and Representatives . . . and the members of the several State Legislatures, and all executive and judicial officers, both of the United States and of the several States, shall be bound by oath or affirmation to support this Constitution.'"[38]

☛ "That the work of the fathers of the republic, that the most magnificent system of constitutional government which the wisdom of man has devised, should be turned from its object, changed from its order, rendered powerless to protect the unalienable rights and sovereignty of the people, and made the instrument by which to establish and maintain imperialism, is a revolution unlike any other that may be found in the history of mankind. The result established the truthfulness of the assertion, so often made during the progress of the war [of 1861], that the Northern people, by their unconstitutional warfare to gain the freedom of certain negro slaves, would lose their own liberties."[39]

☛ "A forced union is a political absurdity. No less absurd is President Lincoln's effort to dissever the sovereignty of the people from that of the State; as if there could be a State without a people, or a sovereign people without a State."[40]

☛ "[We should look] steadily to the Constitution, as the mariner looks to the compass, for guidance . . ."[41]

☛ "The theory of our Constitution . . . is one of peace, of equality of sovereign States. It was made by States and made for States; and for greater assurance they passed an amendment, doing that which was necessarily implied by the nature of the instrument, as it was a mere instrument of grants. But, in the abundance of caution, they declared that everything which had not been delegated was reserved to the States, or to the people—that is, to the State governments as instituted by the people of each State, or to the people in their sovereign capacity."[42]

☛ "[It is a historical fact that] the States of which the American Union was formed, from the moment when they emerged from their colonial or provincial condition, became, severally, sovereign, free, and independent States—not one State or Nation;

"That the Union formed under the Articles of Confederation was a compact between the States in which these attributes of sovereignty, freedom, and independence were expressly asserted and guaranteed;

"That in forming 'the more perfect Union' of the Constitution afterward adopted, the same contracting powers formed an amended compact, without any surrender of these attributes, either expressed or implied; but, on the contrary, by the Tenth Amendment to the Constitution, limiting the authority of the Federal Government to its express grants, with a distinct provision against the presumption of a surrender of anything by implication . . ."[43]

☛ "[It is a historical fact that] political sovereignty, in contradistinction to the natural rights of man, resides neither in the individual citizen, nor in unorganized masses, nor in fractional subdivisions of a community, but in the people of an organized political body;

"That no 'republican form of government,' in the sense in which that expression is used in the Constitution, and was generally understood by the founders of the Union—whether it be the government of a State or of a Confederation of States—is possessed of any sovereignty whatever, but merely exercises certain powers delegated by the sovereign authority of the people, and subject to recall and resumption by the same authority that conferred them;

"That the 'people' who organized the first [U.S.] Confederation [in 1781], the people who dissolved it, the people who ordained and established the Constitution which succeeded it—the only people known or referred to in the phraseology of that period—were the people of the respective States, each acting separately and with absolute independence of the others . . ."[44]

☛ "[It is a historical fact that] in forming and adopting the Constitution, the States, or the people of the States, formed a new Government but no new People, and that, consequently, no new sovereignty was created; for sovereignty, in an American republic, can belong only to a People, never to a Government; and that the Federal Government is entitled to exercise only the powers delegated to it by the people of the several States.

"That the term People in the preamble to the Constitution and in the tenth Amendment, is used distributively; that the only 'People of the United States' known to the Constitution are the people of each State in the Union; that no such political community or corporate unit as one people of the United States then existed, has ever been organized, or yet exists; and that no political action by the people of the United States in the aggregate has ever taken place, or ever can take place under the Constitution."[45]

☛ "These [constitutional] principles, although they had come to be considered as peculiarly Southern, were not sectional in their origin. In the beginning and earlier years of our history they were cherished as faithfully and guarded as jealously in Massachusetts and New Hampshire as in Virginia and South Carolina.

"It was in these principles that I was nurtured."[46]

☛ ". . . my father and my uncles fought through the Revolution of 1776, giving their youth, their blood, and their little patrimony to the constitutional freedom which I claim as my inheritance. Three of my brothers fought in the war of 1812. Two of them were comrades of the Hero of the Hermitage [Andrew Jackson], and received his commendation for gallantry at New Orleans. At sixteen years of age I was given to the service of my country [the U.S.A.]; for twelve years of my life I have borne its arms and served it zealously, if not well.

". . . I have often asserted the right, for which the battles of the Revolution were fought—the right of a people to change their government whenever it was found to be oppressive, and subversive of the objects for which governments are instituted—and have contended for the independence and sovereignty of the States, a part of the creed of which Jefferson was the apostle, Madison the expounder, and Jackson the consistent defender."[47]

☛ "It has been shown that the governments of the States were instituted to secure certain unalienable rights of the citizens with which they were endowed by their Creator, and that among these rights were life, liberty, and the pursuit of happiness; that they derived their just powers from the consent of the governed; and that these powers were organized by the citizens in such form as seemed to them most likely to effect their safety and happiness. Where must the American citizen look for the security of the rights with which he has been endowed by his Creator? To his State government. Where shall he look to find security and protection for his life, security and protection for his personal liberty, security and protection for his property, security and protection for his safety and happiness? Only to his State government."[48]

Davis' brief definition of the U.S. Constitution:
☛ ". . . a compact the binding force of which is based upon the sovereignty of the states . . ."[49]

Davis' more detailed definition of the U.S. Constitution:
☛ "The whole body of the instrument, the history of its formation and adoption, as well as the tenth amendment, added in an abundance of caution, clearly show it to be an instrument enumerating the powers delegated by the States to the Federal Government, their common agent. It is specifically declared that all which was not so delegated was reserved. On this mass of reserved powers, those which the States declined to grant, the Federal Government was expressly forbidden to intrude."[50]

☛ "The ultimate ownership of the soil, or eminent domain, remains with the people of the state in which it lies, by virtue of their sovereignty."[51]

☛ "He must have been a careless reader of our political history who has not observed that, whether under the style of 'United Colonies' or 'United States,' which was adopted after the Declaration of Independence, whether under the articles of Confederation or the compact of Union, there everywhere appears the distinct assertion of State sovereignty, and nowhere the slightest suggestion of any purpose on the part of the States to consolidate themselves into one body. Will any candid, well-informed man assert that, at any time between 1776 and 1790, a proposition to surrender the sovereignty of the States and merge them in a central government would have had the least possible chance of adoption? Can any historical fact be more demonstrable than that the States did, both in the Confederation [1781 to 1789] and in the Union [post 1789], retain their sovereignty and independence as distinct communities, voluntarily consenting to federation, but never becoming the fractional parts of a nation? That such opinions should find adherents in our day, may be attributable to the natural law of aggregation; surely not to a conscientious regard for the terms of the compact for union by the States.

"In all free governments the constitution or organic law is supreme over the government, and in our Federal Union this was most distinctly marked by limitations and prohibitions against all which was beyond the expressed grants of power to the General Government. In the foreground, therefore, I take the position that those who resisted violations of the compact were the true friends, and those who maintained the usurpation of undelegated powers were the real enemies of the constitutional Union."[52]

☛ "The duty of the State government is to give to its citizens perfect and complete security. It is necessarily sovereign within its own domain, for it is the representative and the constituted agent of the inherent sovereignty of the individuals. For the performance of its duty of protection it may unite with other sovereignties; and also, for better safety and security to its citizens, it may withdraw or secede from such Union."[53]

☛ "In comparing the past and the present among the mighty changes which passion and sectional hostility have wrought, one is profoundly and painfully impressed by the extent to which public opinion has drifted from the landmarks set up by the sages and patriots who formed the constitutional Union, and observed by those who administered its government down to the time when war between the States was inaugurated. Mr. [James] Buchanan, the last President of the old school, would as soon have thought of aiding in the establishment of a monarchy among us as of accepting the doctrine of coercing the States into submission to the will of a majority, in mass, of the people of the United States."[54]

When attacked in the U.S. Senate for allegedly wanting to "spread slavery" into the Western Territories, Davis replied:
☛ "We, sir, have not asked that slavery should be established in California. We have only asked that there should be no restriction; that climate and soil should be left free to establish the institution or not, as experience should determine."[55]

☛ "Among the great purposes declared in the preamble of the Constitution is one to provide for the general welfare. Provision for the general welfare implies general fraternity. This Union was not expected to be held together by coercion; the power of force as a means was denied. They sought, however, to bind it perpetually together with that which was stronger than triple bars of brass and steel   the ceaseless current of kind offices, renewing and renewed in an eternal flow, and gathering volume and velocity as it rolled. It was a function intended not for the injury of any. It declared its purpose to be the benefit of all."[56]

☛ ". . . the tenth amendment of the Constitution declared that all which had not been delegated was reserved to the States or to the people. Now, I ask, where among the delegated grants to the Federal Government do you find any power to coerce a State; where among the provisions of the Constitution do you find any prohibition on the part of a State to withdraw; and, if you find neither one nor the other, must not this power be in that great depository, the reserved rights of the States? How was it ever taken out of that source of all power to be given to the Federal Government? It was not delegated to the Federal Government; it was not prohibited to the States; it necessarily remains, then, among the reserved powers of the States."[57]

☞ "The people never have separated themselves from those rights which our fathers had declared to be unalienable. They did not delegate to the Federal Government the powers which the British Crown exercised over the colonies; they did not achieve their independence for any purpose so low as that. They left us to the inheritance of freemen, living in independent communities, the States united for the purposes which they thought would bless posterity."[58]

☞ "If I must have revolution, I say let it be a revolution such as our fathers made when they were denied their natural rights."[59]

☞ "Whatever may be the result [of the impending war with the North], impartial history will record the innocence of the Government of the Confederate States, and place the responsibility of the blood and mourning that may ensue upon those who have denied the great fundamental doctrine of American liberty, that 'governments derive their just powers from the consent of the governed,' and who have set naval and land armaments in motion to subject the people of one portion of this land to the will of another portion."[60]

☞ "The objects which . . . [the U.S. Constitution] was designed to secure to the States and their people were of a truly peaceful nature, and commended themselves to the approbation of men. They were stated by its authors in a form called 'the preamble' of their work, which is in these words: 'We, the people of the United States, in order to form a more perfect union, establish justice, insure domestic tranquillity, provide for the common defense, promote the general welfare, and secure the blessings of liberty to ourselves and our posterity, do ordain and establish this Constitution of the United States.'

"Mankind must contemplate with horror the fact that an organization established for such peaceful and benign ends did, within the first century of its existence, lead the assault in a civil war that brought nearly four millions of soldiers into the field, destroyed thousands and thousands of millions of treasure, trampled the unalienable rights of the people under foot, subverted and subjugated the governments of the States, and ended by establishing itself as supreme and sovereign over all."[61]

☞ "[It is a fact that the delegates to the Convention of 1787] were sent for the 'sole and express purpose' of revising the Articles of Confederation and devising means for rendering the Federal Constitution 'adequate to the exigencies of government and the preservation of the Union'; that the terms 'Union,' 'United States,' 'Federal Constitution,' and 'Constitution of the Federal Government,' were applied to the old Confederation [of 1781] in precisely the same sense in which they are used under the new; that the proposition to constitute a 'national' Government was distinctly rejected by the Convention; that the right of any State, or States, to withdraw from union with the others was practically exemplified, and that the idea of coercion of a State, or compulsory measures, was distinctly excluded under any construction that can be put upon the action of the Convention."[62]

☞ "Which is the higher authority, Lincoln . . . or the Constitution? If the former, then what are constitutions worth for the protection of rights?"[63]

3

THE UNITED STATES
& HER GOVERNMENT

☞ "Our State governments have charge of nearly all the relations of person and property. This Federal [that is, central] Government was instituted mainly as a common agent for foreign purposes, for free trade among the States, and for common defense."[64]

☞ "One of the fruitful sources, as I hold it, of the errors which prevail in our country, is the theory that this is a Government of one people; that the Government of the United States was formed by a mass. The Government of the United States is a compact between the sovereign members who formed it; and, if there be one feature common to all the colonies planted upon the shores of America, it is desire for community independence."[65]

Davis sitting in his favorite spot: a bench on the waterfront at his Biloxi, Mississippi, home "Beauvoir."

☞ ". . . the united colonies, when they declared their independence, formed a league or alliance with one another as 'United States.' This title antedated the adoption of the Articles of Confederation [in 1781]. It was assumed immediately after the Declaration of Independence, and was continued under the Articles of Confederation; the first of which declared that 'the style of this confederacy shall be *The United States of America*'; and this style was retained—without question—in the formation of the present Constitution. The name was not adopted as antithetical to, or distinctive from, 'confederate,' as some seem to have imagined. If it has any significance now, it must have had the same under the Articles of Confederation, or even before they were adopted.

". . . the States which thus became and continued to be 'united,' whatever form their union assumed, acted and continued to act as distinct and sovereign political communities. The monstrous fiction that they acted as one people 'in their aggregate capacity' has not an atom of fact to serve as a basis."[66]

☞ "When the colonies united in sending representatives to a Congress in Philadelphia [in 1787], there was no purpose—no suggestion of a purpose—to merge their separate individuality in one consolidated mass. No such idea existed, or with their known opinions could have existed. They did not assume to become a united colony or province, but styled themselves 'united colonies'—colonies united for purposes of mutual counsel and defense, as the New England colonies had been united more than a hundred years before. It was as 'United States'—not as a state, or united people—that these colonies—still distinct and politically independent of each other—asserted and achieved their independence of the mother-country. As 'United States' they adopted the Articles of Confederation, in which the separate sovereignty, freedom, and independence of each was distinctly asserted. They were 'united States' when Great Britain acknowledged the absolute freedom and independence of each, distinctly and separately recognized by name. France and Spain were parties to the same treaty, and the French and Spanish idioms still express and perpetuate, more exactly than the English, the true idea intended to be embodied in the title—*les États Unis*, or *los Estados Unidos*—the *States united*.

"It was without any change of title—still as 'United States'—without any sacrifice of individuality—without any compromise of sovereignty—that the same parties entered into a new and amended compact with one another under the present Constitution. Larger and more varied powers were conferred upon the common Government for the purpose of insuring 'a more perfect union'—not for that of destroying or impairing the integrity of the contracting members."[67]

☛ ". . . in all these changes of circumstances and of government, there has never been one single instance of action by the 'people of the United States in the aggregate,' or as one body. Before the era of independence, whatever was done by the people of the colonies was done by the people of each colony separately and independently of each other, although in union by their delegates for certain specified purposes. Since the assertion of their independence [from Britain], the people of the United States have never acted otherwise than as the people of each State, severally and separately."[68]

☛ "[The Constitution] was never submitted to 'the people of the United States in the aggregate,' or as a people. Indeed, no such political community as the people of the United States in the aggregate exists at this day or ever did exist. Senators in Congress confessedly represent the States as equal units. The House of Representatives is not a body of representatives of 'the people of the United States,' as often erroneously asserted; but the Constitution, in the second section of its first article, expressly declares that it 'shall be composed of members chosen by the people of the several States.'"[69]

☛ "Nor is it true that the President and Vice-President are elected, as it is sometimes vaguely stated, by vote of the 'whole people' of the Union. Their election is even more unlike what such a vote would be than that of the representatives, who in numbers at least represent the strength of their respective States. In the election of President and Vice-President the Constitution (Article II) prescribes that '*each State* shall appoint, in such manner as the Legislature thereof may direct, a number of electors' [the Electoral College] for the purpose of choosing a President and Vice-President. The number of these electors is based partly upon the equal sovereignty, partly upon the unequal population of the respective States."[70]

☛ "It is, then, absolutely true that there has never been any such thing as a vote of 'the people of the United States in the aggregate'; no such people is recognized by the Constitution; and no such political community has ever existed. It is equally true that no officer or department of the General Government formed by the Constitution derives authority from a majority of the whole people of the United States, or has ever been chosen by such majority. As little as any other is the United States Government a government of a majority of the mass."[71]

☞ "[According to constitutional principles] . . . seventy thousand people in the State of Delaware had precisely the same weight—one vote—in its ratification, as seven hundred thousand (and more) in Virginia, or four hundred thousand in Pennsylvania. Would not this have been an intolerable grievance and wrong—would no protest have been uttered against it—if these had been fractional parts of one community of people?

"Again, while the will of the consenting majority within any State was binding on the opposing minority in the same, no majority, or majorities, of States or people had any control whatever upon the people of another State. The Constitution was established, not 'over the States' . . . but 'between the States,' and only 'between the States so ratifying the same.' Little Rhode Island, with her seventy thousand inhabitants, was not a mere fractional part of 'the people of the whole land,' during the period for which she held aloof, but was as free, independent, and unmolested, as any other sovereign power, notwithstanding the majority of more than three millions of 'the whole people' on the other side of the question."[72]

When asked about President Lincoln's ultimate goal to rule the South with either "bullets or ballots":
☞ "We [Southerners] seceded to rid ourselves of the rule of the majority . . . Neither current events nor history show that the majority rules, or ever did rule. The contrary, I think, is true. . . . the states are independent and sovereign. The country is not. It is only a Confederation of states, or rather it was; it is now *two* confederations."[73]

☞ "The Government of the United States is like no other government. It is neither a 'constitutional republic or democracy,' nor has it ever been thus called. Neither is it a 'government of the people by the same people'; but it is known and designated as 'the Government of the United States.' It is an anomaly among governments. Its authority consists solely of certain powers delegated to it, as a common agent, by an association of sovereign and independent States. These powers are to be exercised only for certain specified objects; and the purposes, declared in the beginning of the deed or instrument of delegation, were 'to form a more perfect union, establish justice, insure domestic tranquillity, provide for the common defense, promote the general welfare, and secure the blessings of liberty to ourselves and our posterity.'"[74]

On the 19ᵗʰ-Century Liberal's idea of "internal improvements," or what is now called corporate welfare:

☛ "Nothing could be more fatal to the independence of the people and the liberties of the States than dependence for support upon the public Treasury, whether it be in the form of subsidies, of bounties, or restrictions on trade for the benefit of special interests. In the decline of the Roman Empire, the epoch in which the hopelessness of renovation was made manifest was that in which the people accepted corn from the public granaries: it preceded but a little the time when the post of emperor became a matter of purchase. How far would it differ from this if [our American] constituencies should choose their representatives, not for their integrity, not for their capacity, not for their past services, but because of their ability to get money from the public Treasury for the benefit of their local interests; and how far would it differ from a purchase of the office if a President were chosen because of the favor he would show to certain moneyed interests?"[75]

☛ "It was by the slow and barely visible approaches of the serpent seeking its prey that the aggressions and usurpations of the United States Government moved on to the crimes against the law of the Union, the usages of war among civilized nations, the dictates of humanity and the requirements of justice . . . The performance of this task has been painful, but persistent and widespread misrepresentation of the cause and conduct of the South required the exposure of her slanderer. To unmask the hypocrisy of claiming devotion to the Constitution, while violating its letter and spirit for a purpose palpably hostile to it, was needful for the defense of the South. [It will one day] be seen how often we have been charged with the very offenses committed by our enemy—offenses of which the South was entirely innocent, and of which a chivalrous people would be incapable. There was in this the old trick of the fugitive thief who cries 'Stop thief!' as he runs."[76]

☛ "The government of the United States adopted a fiction when it declared that the execution of the laws in certain states was impeded by 'insurrection.' . . . [Why] did an intelligent and powerful Government, like that of the United States, so outrage the understanding of mankind as to adopt a fiction on which to base the authority and justification of its hostile action? The United States Government is the result of a compact between the States—a written Constitution. It owes its existence simply to a delegation of certain powers by the respective States, which it is authorized to exercise for their common welfare. One of these powers is to 'suppress insurrections'; but there is no power delegated to subjugate States, the authors of its existence, or to make war on any of the States. If, then, without any delegated power or lawful authority for its proceedings, the Government of the United States commenced a war upon some of the States of the Union, how could it expect to be justified before the world? It became the aggressor—the Attila of the American Continent. Its action inflicted a wound on the principles of constitutional liberty, a crushing blow to the hopes that men had begun to repose in this latest effort for self-government, which its friends should never forgive nor ever forget."[77]

☛ "To palliate the enormity of such an offense, its [Yankee] authors resorted to a vehement denial that their hostile action was a war upon the States, and persistently asserted the fiction that their immense armies and fleets were merely a police authority to put down insurrection. They hoped to conceal from the observation of the American people that the contest, on the part of the central Government, was for empire, for its absolute supremacy over the State governments; that the Constitution was rolled up and laid away among the old archives; and that the conditions of their liberty, in the future, were to be decided by the sword or by 'national' control of the ballot-box."[78]

☛ ". . . I have long since said that I could put no faith in politicians."[79]

The Confederate Capitol at Montgomery, Alabama. Later, in May 1861, Davis had the Confederacy's capital moved to Richmond, Virginia.

4

THE UNION

☞ "This Union is dear to me as a Union of fraternal States. It would lose its value if I had to regard it as a Union held together by physical force."[80]

On the true meaning of the term 'perpetual union':
☞ ". . . a number of 'sovereign, free, and independent' States, during the war of the [American] Revolution, entered into a partnership with one another [known, from 1781 to 1789, as the 'Confederacy'], which was not only unlimited in duration, but expressly declared to be a 'perpetual union.' Yet, when that Union failed to accomplish the purposes for which it was formed, the parties withdrew, separately and independently, one after another, without any question made of their right to do so, and formed a new association. One of the declared objects of this new partnership was to form 'a more perfect union.' This certainly did not mean more perfect in respect of duration; for the former union had been declared perpetual, and perpetuity admits of no addition. It did not mean that it was to be more indissoluble . . . It was an amended Union, not a consolidation."[81]

Davis at "Beauvoir."

☞ "Now for the first time, we are about permanently to destroy the balance of power between the sections of the Union, by securing a majority to one, in both Houses of Congress . . . When that barrier for the protection of the minority is about to be obliterated, I feel we have reached the point at which the decline of our Government has commenced . . ."[82]

On why the words 'secede' and 'secession' do not appear in the U.S. Constitution:
☞ "It was not necessary in the Constitution to affirm the right of secession, because it was an attribute of sovereignty, and the states had reserved all which they had not delegated [to the central government]."[83]

☞ "The [U.S.] Constitution did not, like the [earlier] Articles of Confederation, declare that the States had agreed to a perpetual union, but distinctly indicated the hope of its perpetuity by the expression in the preamble of the purpose to 'secure the blessings of liberty to ourselves and our posterity.' The circumstances under which the Union of the Constitution was formed justified the hope of its perpetuity, but the brief existence of the [U.S.] Confederation [1781 to 1789] may have been a warning against the renewal of the assertion that the compact should be perpetual. . . . Thus was the Union to be a voluntary compact . . ."[84]

☞ "We of the South stand now, as we have always stood, upon the defensive. . . . [The Southern people] know their rights while they feel their wrongs; and they will maintain the one, resent the other, if need be, and preserve our Constitutional Union; but the Union without the Constitution they hold to be a curse. With the Constitution, they will never abandon it. We, sir, are parties to the Union only under the Constitution, and there is no power known in the world that could dictate to my little State a Union in which her rights were continually disregarded and trampled upon by an unrestrained majority. The present generation [of Southerners], sir, all maintain the character their fathers bore. They well know how to sustain the institutions which they inherited, even by civil war, if that be provoked. They will march up to the issue and meet it face to face."[85]

☞ "[We] . . . will resist an odious, unconstitutional, and unjust discrimination against [our] . . . rights. This, sir, is to maintain the Union by preserving the foundation on which it stands; and if it be sedition or treason to raise voice and hand against the miners [that is, Northern Liberals] who are working for its overthrow, against those who are seeking to build upon its ruins a new Union which rests not upon the Constitution for authority, but upon the dominant will of the majority, then my heart is filled with such sedition and treason, and the reproach which it brings is esteemed as an honor."[86]

5

CAUSES OF THE WAR

☛ "[One of the main causes of the War surely was] the ravings of a party in the North [that is, Lincoln's], which denounced the Constitution and the Union, and persistently defamed their brethren of the South."[87]

☛ "Ignorance and credulity have enabled unscrupulous partisans so to mislead public opinion, both at home and abroad, as to create the belief that the institution of African slavery was the chief cause, instead of being a mere incident in the group of causes, which led to war. In keeping with the first misrepresentation was that of the position assigned to the belligerent parties. Thus, the North is represented as having fought for the emancipation of the African slaves, and the South for the increase and extension of the institution of African servitude as it existed in the Southern States. Therein is a twofold fallacy."[88]

Sarah Knox Taylor (1815-1835), Davis' first wife. The daughter of twelfth U.S. President Zachary Taylor (1784-1850) and the elder sister of famed Confederate General Richard Taylor (1826-1879), Sarah is a cousin of the author.

☛ "[Under Lincoln] the states and the people thereof had become consolidated into a national Union. . . . This was the usurpation. This lay at the foundation of the war. Every subsequent act of the Government was another step in the same direction, all tending palpably to supremacy for the Government of the United States, the subjugation of the States, and the submission of the people."[89]

☛ "This was the adversary with whom we had to struggle, and this was the issue for which we fought. That we dared to draw our swords to vindicate the rights and the sovereignty of the people, that we dared to resist and deny all sovereignty as inherently existing in the Government of the United States, was adjudged an infamous crime, and we were denounced as 'rebels.' It was asserted that those of us 'who were captured should be hung as rebels taken in the act.' Crushing the corner-stone of the Union, the independence of the States, the Federal Government assumed toward us a position of haughty arrogance, refused to recognize us otherwise than as insurrectionists and 'rebels,' who resisted and denied its usurped sovereignty, and who were entitled to no amelioration from the punishment of death, except such as might proceed only from the promptings of mercy."[90]

☛ "Under the power of Congress to levy duties on imports, tariff laws were enacted, not merely 'to pay the debts and provide for the common defense and general welfare of the United States,' as authorized by the Constitution, but, positively and primarily, for the protection against foreign competition of domestic manufactures. The effect of this was to impose the main burden of taxation upon the Southern people, who were consumers and not manufacturers, not only by the enhanced price of imports, but indirectly by the consequent depreciation in the value of exports, which were chiefly the products of Southern States. The imposition of this grievance was unaccompanied by the consolation of knowing that the tax thus borne was to be paid into the public Treasury, for the increase of price accrued mainly to the benefit of the manufacturer. Nor was this all: a reference to the annual appropriations will show that the disbursements made were as unequal as the burdens borne— the inequality in both operating in the same direction.

"These causes all combined to direct immigration to the Northern section; and with the increase of its preponderance appeared more and more distinctly a tendency in the Federal Government to pervert functions delegated to it, and to use them with sectional discrimination against the [Southern] minority."[91]

☛ "[More proof that slavery was not the cause of the War comes from the Lincoln Government itself.] As late as the 22d of April, 1861, Mr. [William Henry] Seward, United States Secretary of State, in a dispatch to [New Jersey Senator] Mr. [William Lewis] Dayton, Minister to France, since made public, expressed the views and purposes of the United States Government in the premises as follows. It may be proper to explain that, by what he is pleased to term 'the revolution,' Mr. Seward means the withdrawal of the

Southern States; and that the words italicized are, perhaps, not so distinguished in the original. He says: 'The Territories will remain in all respects the same, whether the revolution shall succeed or shall fail. *The condition of slavery in the several States will remain just the same, whether it succeed or fail.* There is not even a pretext for the complaint that the disaffected States are to be conquered by the United States if the revolution fails; for the rights of the States and *the condition of every being in them* will remain subject to exactly the same laws and forms of administration, whether the revolution shall succeed or whether it shall fail. In the one case, the States would be federally connected with the new Confederacy; in the other, they would, as now, be members of the United States; *but their Constitutions and laws, customs, habits, and institutions, in either case, will remain the same.*'"[92]

☛ "By the exclusion of the South, in 1820, from all that part of the Louisiana purchase lying north of the parallel of thirty-six degrees thirty minutes, and not included in the State of Missouri; by the extension of that line of exclusion to embrace the territory acquired from Texas; and by the appropriation of all the territory obtained from Mexico under the Treaty of Guadalupe Hidalgo, both north and south of that line, it may be stated with approximate accuracy that the North had monopolized to herself more than three fourths of all that had been added to the domain of the United States since the Declaration of Independence. This inequality, which began . . . in the more generous than wise confidence of the South, was employed to obtain for the North the lion's share of what was afterward added at the cost of the public treasure and the blood of patriots."[93]

☛ "Nor was this the only cause that operated to disappoint the reasonable hopes and to blight the fair prospects under which the original compact was formed. The effects of discriminating duties upon imports . . . favoring the manufacturing region, which was the North; burdening the exporting region, which was the South; and so imposing upon the latter a double tax: one, by the increased price of articles of consumption, which, so far as they were of home production, went into the pockets of the manufacturer; the other, by the diminished value of articles of export, which was so much withheld from the pockets of the agriculturist. In like manner the power of the majority section was employed to appropriate to itself an unequal share of the public disbursements. These combined causes—the possession of more territory, more money, and a wider field for the employment of special labor—all served to attract immigration; and, with increasing population, the greed grew by what it fed on."[94]

☛ "This became distinctly manifest when the so-called 'Republican' [that is, the Liberal Party of that day] Convention assembled in Chicago, on May 16, 1860, to nominate a candidate for the Presidency. It was a purely sectional body. There were a few delegates present, representing an insignificant minority in the 'border States,' Delaware, Maryland, Virginia, Kentucky, and Missouri; but not one from any State south of the celebrated political line of thirty-six degrees thirty minutes. It had been the invariable usage with nominating conventions of all parties to select candidates for the Presidency and Vice-Presidency, one from the North and the other from the South; but this assemblage nominated Mr. Lincoln, of Illinois, for the first office, and for the second, Mr. [Hannibal] Hamlin, of Maine—both Northerners. Mr. Lincoln, its nominee for the Presidency, had publicly announced that the Union 'could not permanently endure, half slave and half free.' The resolutions adopted contained some carefully worded declarations, well adapted to deceive the credulous who were opposed to hostile aggressions upon the rights of the States. In order to accomplish this purpose, they were compelled to create a fictitious issue, in denouncing what they described as 'the new dogma that the Constitution, of its own force, carries slavery into any or all of the Territories of the United States'—a 'dogma' which had never been held or declared by anybody, and which had no existence outside of their own assertion. There was enough in connection with the nomination to assure the most fanatical foes of the Constitution that their ideas would be the rule and guide of the party."[95]

☛ "The resistance to the admission of Missouri as a State, in 1820, was evidently not owing to any moral or constitutional considerations, but merely to political motives; and the compensation exacted for granting what was simply a right, was the exclusion of the South from equality in the enjoyment of territory which justly belonged equally to both, and which was what the enemies of the South stigmatized as 'slave territory,' when acquired."[96]

☛ "The sectional policy then indicated brought to its support the passions that spring from man's higher nature, but which, like all passions, if misdirected and perverted, become hurtful and, it may be, destructive. The year 1835 was marked by the public agitation for the abolition of that African servitude which existed in the South, which antedated the Union, and had existed in every one of the States that formed the [U.S.] Confederation [of 1781]. By a great misconception of the powers belonging to the General Government, and the responsibilities of citizens of the Northern States, many of those citizens were, little by little, brought to the conclusion that slavery was a sin for which they were answerable; and that it was the duty of the Federal Government to abate it."[97]

☛ "Thus, by the activity of the propagandists of abolitionism, and the misuse of the sacred word Liberty, they recruited from the ardent worshipers of that goddess such numbers as gave them in many Northern States the balance of power between the two great political forces that stood arrayed against each other; then and there they came to be courted by both of the great parties, especially by the Whigs [essentially the big government Liberals of the day], who had become the weaker party of the two. Fanaticism, to which is usually accorded sincerity as an extenuation of its mischievous tenets, affords the best excuse to be offered for the original abolitionists, but that can not be conceded to the political associates who joined them for the purpose of acquiring power; with them it was but hypocritical cant, intended to deceive. Hence arose the declaration of the existence of an 'irrepressible conflict,' because of the domestic institutions of sovereign, self-governing States—institutions over which neither the Federal Government nor the people outside of the limits of such States had any control, and for which they could have no moral or legal responsibility."[98]

☛ "These facts prove incontestably that the sectional hostility which exhibited itself in 1820, on the application of Missouri for admission into the Union, which again broke out on the proposition for the annexation of Texas in 1844, and which reappeared after the Mexican war, never again to be suppressed until its fell results had been fully accomplished, was not the consequence of any difference on the abstract question of slavery. It was the offspring of sectional rivalry and political ambition. It would have manifested itself just as certainly if slavery had existed in all the States, or if there had not been a [single] negro in America. No such pretension was made in 1803 or 1811, when the Louisiana purchase, and afterward the admission into the Union of the State of that name, elicited threats of disunion from the representatives of New England. The complaint was not of slavery, but of 'the acquisition of more weight at the other extremity' of the Union. [As now, it] was not slavery that threatened a rupture in 1832, but the unjust and unequal operation of a protective tariff."[99]

☛ "The raid into Virginia under John Brown—already notorious as a fanatical partisan leader in the Kansas troubles—occurred in October, 1859, a few weeks before the meeting of the Thirty-sixth Congress. Insignificant in itself and in its immediate results, it afforded a startling revelation of the extent to which sectional hatred and political fanaticism had blinded the conscience of a class of persons in certain States of the Union; forming a party steadily growing stronger in numbers, as well as in activity."[100]

☛ "[Just prior to the 1860 presidential election, it] needed but little knowledge of the status of parties in the several States to foresee a probable defeat if the conservatives [known as the Democrats at the time] were to continue divided into three parts, and the aggressives [that is, progressives: the liberal pro-North candidates and their supporters] were to be held in solid column. But angry passions, which are always bad counselors, had been aroused, and hopes were still cherished, which proved to be illusory. The result was the election, by a minority, of a President [that is, Lincoln] whose avowed principles were necessarily fatal to the harmony of the Union."[101]

☛ "[Between 1850 and 1860] the progress of sectional discord and the tendency of the stronger section to unconstitutional aggression had been fearfully rapid. With very rare exceptions, there were none in 1850 who claimed the right of the Federal Government to apply coercion to a State. In 1860 men had grown to be familiar with threats of driving the South into submission to any act that the Government, in the hands of a Northern majority, might see fit to perform. During the canvass of that year, demonstrations had been made by quasi-military organizations in various parts of the North, which looked unmistakably to purposes widely different from those enunciated in the preamble to the Constitution, and to the employment of means not authorized by the powers which the States had delegated to the Federal Government."[102]

☛ "Well-informed men still remembered that, in the [1787] Convention which framed the Constitution, a proposition was made to authorize the employment of force against a delinquent State, on which Mr. [James] Madison remarked that 'the use of force against a State would look more like a declaration of war than an infliction of punishment, and would probably be considered by the party attacked as a dissolution of all previous compacts by which it might have been bound.' The Convention expressly refused to confer the power proposed, and the clause was lost. While, therefore, in 1860, many violent men, appealing to passion and the lust of power, were inciting the multitude, and preparing Northern opinion to support a war waged against the Southern States in the event of their secession, there were others who took a different view of the case. Notable among such was . . . [Yankee crusader Horace Greeley's] *New York Tribune*, which had been the organ of the abolitionists, and which now declared that, 'if the cotton States wished to withdraw from the Union, they should be allowed to do so'; that 'any attempt to compel them to remain, by force, would be contrary to the principles of the Declaration of Independence and to the fundamental ideas upon which human liberty is based'; and that, 'if the Declaration of Independence justified the secession from the British Empire of three millions of subjects in 1776, it was not seen why it would not justify the secession of five millions of Southerners from the Union in 1861.' Again, it was said by the same journal that, 'sooner than compromise with the South and abandon the Chicago platform,' they would 'let the Union slide.' Taunting expressions were freely used—as, for example, 'If the Southern people wish to leave the Union, we will do our best to forward their views.'"[103]

☛ "That signs of coming danger so visible, evidences of hostility so unmistakable, disregard of constitutional obligations so wanton, taunts and jeers so bitter and insulting, should serve to increase excitement in the South, was a consequence flowing as much from reason and patriotism as from sentiment. He must have been ignorant of human nature who did not expect such a tree to bear fruits of discord and division."[104]

6

SECESSION

☞ "In the words of the Declaration of Independence: 'We hold these truths to be self-evident, that, whenever any form of government becomes destructive of these ends [life, liberty, and the pursuit of happiness], it is the right of the people to alter or to abolish it, and to institute a new government, laying its foundation on such principles, and organizing its powers in such form, as to them shall seem most likely to effect their safety and happiness. . . . When a long train of abuses and usurpations, pursuing invariably the same object, evinces a design to reduce them under absolute despotism, it is their right, it is their duty, to throw off such government, and to provide new guards for their future security.'"[105]

Sketch of Davis and part of his family. Left to right: Margaret Howell Davis (1855-1909), Jefferson Hayes (1884-1975), Jefferson Davis (1808-1889), Varina Ann Howell Jefferson Davis (1864-1898), Varina Banks Howell (1826-1905).

A warning to Yankee politicians:
☞ "Senators of the North, you are reënacting the blunders which statesmen in Great Britain committed [in 1775] . . ."[106]

☞ ". . . if war should come, if we must again baptize in blood the principles for which our fathers bled in the [American] Revolution, we shall show we are not degenerate sons, but will redeem the pledges they gave, preserve the sacred rights they transmitted to us, and show that Southern valor still shines as brightly as in 1776, in 1812, and in every other conflict."[107]

☛ "One of the incidents that led to our withdrawal from the Union was the apprehension that it was the intention of the United States Government to violate the constitutional right of each State to adopt and maintain, to reject or abolish slavery, as it pleased."[108]

☛ "Such a [U.S.] government as ours had no power to maintain its existence any longer than the contracting parties pleased to cohere, because it was founded on the great principle of voluntary federation, and organized 'to establish justice and insure domestic tranquillity.' Any departure from this principle by the General Government not only perverts and destroys its nature, but furnishes a just cause to the injured State to withdraw from the union. A new union might subsequently be formed, but the original one could never by coercion be restored. Any effort on the part of the others to force the seceding State to consent to come back is an attempt at subjugation. It is a wrong which no lapse of time or combination of circumstances can ever make right."[109]

☛ ". . . the North threatened and the South acted."[110]

☛ ". . . I, in common with others, desired to have a peaceful separation, and sent commissioners to the United States Government to effect, if possible, negotiations to that end . . ."[111]

☛ "The plan of the [Confederate] Peace Conference was treated by the majority [of Yankee politicians] with the contemptuous indifference shown to every other [Southern] movement for conciliation. Its mere consideration was objected to by the extreme radicals [that is, the Yankee abolitionists of the Republican Party—the Liberal Party of the day]. . ."[112]

☛ "With the failure of these efforts, which occurred on the eve of the inauguration of Mr. Lincoln, and the accession to power of a party founded on a basis of sectional aggression, and now thoroughly committed to its prosecution and perpetuation, expired the last hopes of reconciliation and union."[113]

☛ "[Under such circumstances, it] might, therefore, have been anticipated that Virginia—one of whose sons wrote the Declaration of Independence, another of whose sons led the armies of the United States in the Revolution which achieved their independence, and another of whose sons mainly contributed to the adoption of the Constitution of the Union—would not have been slow, in the face of such events, to reclaim the grants she had made to the General Government, and to withdraw from the Union, to the establishment of which she had so largely contributed."[114]

☛ "I would be happy to know that every State now felt that fraternity which made this Union possible; and, if that evidence could go out, if evidence satisfactory to the people of the South could be given that that feeling existed in the hearts of the Northern people, you might burn your statute-books and we would cling to the Union still. But it is because of their conviction that hostility, and not fraternity, now exists in the hearts of the people, that they are looking to their reserved rights and to their independent powers for their own protection."[115]

☛ "What resource for justice—what assurance of tranquillity—what guarantee of safety—now remained for the South? Still forbearing, still hoping, still striving for peace and union, we waited until a sectional President, nominated by a sectional convention, elected by a sectional vote—and that the vote of a minority of the people—was about to be inducted into office, under the warning of his own distinct announcement that the Union could not permanently endure 'half slave and half free'; meaning thereby that it could not continue to exist in the condition in which it was formed and its Constitution adopted. The leader of his party [William H. Seward], who was to be the chief of his Cabinet, was the man who had first proclaimed an 'irrepressible conflict' between the North and the South, and who had declared that abolitionism, having triumphed in the Territories, would proceed to the invasion of the States. Even then the Southern people did not finally despair until the temper of the triumphant party had been tested in Congress and found adverse to any terms of reconciliation consistent with the honor and safety of all parties.

"No alternative remained except to seek the security out of the Union which they had vainly tried to obtain within it. The hope of our people may be stated in a sentence. It was to escape from injury and strife in the Union, to find prosperity and peace out of it."[116]

☛ "The alternative to secession is coercion."[117]

☛ "The [Southern] people of the States now confederated became convinced that the Government of the United States had fallen into the hands of a sectional majority, who would pervert that most sacred of all trusts to the destruction of the rights which it was pledged to protect. They believed that to remain longer in the Union would subject them to a continuance of a disparaging discrimination, submission to which would be inconsistent with their welfare, and intolerable to a proud people. They therefore determined to sever its bonds and establish a new Confederacy for themselves."[118]

☛ "The Right of Secession—that subject which, beyond all others, ignorance, prejudice, and political rancor have combined to cloud with misstatements and misapprehensions—is a question easily to be determined in the light of . . . the history and principles of the Constitution. It is not something standing apart by itself—a factious creation, outside of and antagonistic to the Constitution—as might be imagined by one deriving his ideas from the [Northern] political literature most current of late years. So far from being against the Constitution or incompatible with it, we contend that, if the right to secede is not prohibited to the States, and no power to prevent it expressly delegated to the United States, it remains as reserved to the States or the people, from whom all the powers of the General Government were derived."[119]

☛ "If sectional hostility had been engendered by dissimilarity of institutions, and by a mistaken idea of moral responsibilities, and by irreconcilable creeds—if the family could no longer live and grow harmoniously together—by patriarchal teaching older than Christianity, it might have been learned that it was better to part, to part peaceably, and to continue, from one to another, the good offices of neighbors who by sacred memories were forbidden ever to be foes."[120]

☛ "There are some things worse than hanging and extermination. We reckon giving up the right of self-government one of those things."[121]

☛ "Men [today] speak of revolution; and when they say revolution they mean blood. Our fathers meant nothing of the sort. When they spoke of revolution they meant an unalienable right. When they declared as an unalienable right the power of the people to abrogate and modify their form of government whenever it did not answer the ends for which it was established, they did not mean that they were to sustain that by brute force. They meant that it was a right; and force could only be invoked when that right was wrongfully denied. . . . Are we, in this age of civilization and political progress . . . now to roll back the whole current of human thought, and again to return to the mere brute force which prevails between beasts of prey, as the only method of settling questions between men?"[122]

On one of the main reasons the South seceded:

☛ "Though the prevailing sentiment of the Southern people was a cordial attachment to the Union as it was formed by their fathers, their love was for the spirit of the compact, for the liberties it was designed to secure, for the self-government and State sovereignty which had been won by separation from the mother-country, and transmitted to them by their Revolutionary sires as a legacy for their posterity for ever."[123]

☛ "Is it to be supposed . . . that the men who fought the battles of the Revolution for community independence . . . terminated their great efforts by transmitting prosperity to a condition in which they could only gain those rights by force? If so, the blood of the Revolution was shed in vain; no great principles were established; for force was the law of nature before the battles of the Revolution were fought."[124]

☛ ". . . we recur to the principles upon which our [American] Government was founded; and when you deny them, and when you deny us the right to withdraw from a Government which, thus perverted, threatens to be destructive of our rights, we but tread in the path of our fathers when we proclaim our independence and take the hazard. This is done, not in hostility to others, not to injure any section of the country, not even for our own pecuniary benefit, but from the high and solemn motive of defending and protecting the rights we inherited, and which it is our duty to transmit unshorn to our children."[125]

☛ "We protest solemnly, in the face of mankind, that we desire peace at any sacrifice, save that of honor. In independence we seek no conquest, no aggrandizement, no concession of any kind from the States with which we have lately been confederated. All we ask is to be let alone—that those who never held power over us shall not now attempt our subjugation by arms. This we will, we must, resist to the direst extremity. The moment that this pretension is abandoned, the sword will drop from our grasp, and we shall be ready to enter into treaties of amity and commerce that can not but be mutually beneficial. So long as this pretension is maintained, with a firm reliance on that Divine Power which covers with its protection the just cause, we must continue to struggle for our inherent right to freedom, independence, and self-government."[126]

☛ "[Secession is] the assertion of the inalienable right of a people to change their government, whenever it ceased to fulfill the purposes for which it was ordained and established. Under our form of government, and the cardinal principles upon which it was founded, it should have been a peaceful remedy. The withdrawal of a State from a league has no revolutionary or insurrectionary characteristic. The government of the State remains unchanged as to all internal affairs. It is only its external or confederate relations that are altered. To term this action of a sovereign a 'rebellion,' is a gross abuse of language. So is the flippant phrase which speaks of it as an appeal to the 'arbitrament of the sword.' In the late contest [that is, Lincoln's "Civil War"], in particular, there was no appeal by the seceding States to the arbitrament of arms. There was on their part no invitation nor provocation to war. They stood in an attitude of self-defense, and were attacked for merely exercising a right guaranteed by the original terms of the compact. They neither tendered nor accepted any challenge to the wager of battle. The man who defends his house against attack can not with any propriety be said to have submitted the question of his right to it to the arbitrament of arms."[127]

On the desire of the people of Massachusetts to, at one time, secede from the Union:
☛ "I well remember an occasion when Massachusetts was arraigned before the bar of the Senate, and when the doctrine of coercion was rife, and to be applied against her, because of the rescue of a fugitive slave in Boston. My opinion then was the same that it is now. Not in a spirit of egotism, but to show that I am not influenced in my opinions because the case is my own, I refer to that time and that occasion as containing the opinion which I then entertained, and on which my present conduct is based. I then said that if Massachusetts—following her purpose through a stated line of conduct—chose to take the last step, which separates her from the Union, it is her right to go, and I will neither vote one dollar nor one man to coerce her back; but I will say to her, Godspeed, in memory of the kind associations which once existed between her and the other States."[128]

☛ "Two moral obligations or restrictions upon a seceding State certainly exist: in the first place, not to break up the partnership without good and sufficient cause; and, in the second, to make an equitable settlement with former associates, and, as far as may be, to avoid the infliction of loss or damage upon any of them. Neither of these obligations was violated or neglected by the Southern States in their secession."[129]

On the general reasons for the Southern secession from the Union:
☛ "When [after] a long course of class legislation, directed not to the general welfare, but to the aggrandizement of the Northern section of the Union, culminated in a warfare on the domestic institutions of the Southern States; when the dogmas of a sectional party, substituted for the provisions of the constitutional compact, threatened to destroy the sovereign rights of the States, [the Southern] . . . States, withdrawing from the Union, confederated together to exercise the right and perform the duty of instituting a government which would better secure the liberties for the preservation of which that Union was established."[130]

☛ "Secession belongs to a different class of remedies. It is to be justified upon the basis that the States are Sovereign. There was a time when none denied it. I hope the time may come again, when a better comprehension of the theory of our Government, and the inalienable rights of the people of the States, will prevent any one from denying that each State is a Sovereign, and thus may reclaim the grants which it has made to any agent whomsoever."[131]

☛ "Sad as have been the consequences of the war which followed secession—disastrous in its moral, material, and political relations—still we have good cause to feel proud that the course of the Southern States has left no blot nor stain upon the honor and chivalry of their people."[132]

7

ANTI-SOUTH PROPAGANDA

☛ "By the reiteration of such unappropriate terms as 'rebellion' and 'treason,' and the asseveration that the South was levying war against the United States, those ignorant of the nature of the Union, and of the reserved powers of the States, have been led to believe that the Confederate States were in the condition of revolted provinces, and that the United States were forced to resort to arms for the preservation of their existence. To those who knew that the Union was formed for specific enumerated purposes, and that the States had never surrendered their sovereignty, it was a palpable absurdity to apply to them, or to their citizens when obeying their mandates, the terms 'rebellion' and 'treason'; and, further . . . the Confederate States, so far from making war or seeking to destroy the United States, as soon as they had an official organ, strove earnestly, by peaceful recognition, to equitably adjust all questions growing out of the separation from their late associates."[133]

Davis' second wife, Confederate First Lady Varina Banks Howell (1826-1905).

☛ "On my way to Montgomery [in early 1861, to assume my position as president of the new Confederacy], brief addresses were made at various places, at which there were temporary stoppages of the trains, in response to calls from the crowds assembled at such points. Some of these addresses were grossly misrepresented in sensational reports made by irresponsible persons, which were published in Northern newspapers, and were not considered worthy of correction under the pressure of the momentous duties then devolving upon me. These false reports, which represented me as invoking war and threatening devastation of the North, have since been adopted by partisan writers as authentic history. It is a sufficient answer to these accusations to refer to my farewell address to the Senate, already given, as reported for the press at the time, and, in connection therewith, to my inaugural address at Montgomery, on assuming the office of President of the Confederate States, on the 18th of February. These two addresses, delivered at an interval of a month, during which no material change of circumstances had occurred, being one before and the other after the date of the sensational reports referred to, are sufficient to stamp them as utterly untrue."[134]

☛ "[The bloodless bombardment and Yankee surrender of Fort Sumter on April 13, 1861,] was seized upon to inflame the mind of the Northern people, and the disguise which had been worn in the communications with the Confederate Commissioners was now thrown off, and it was cunningly attempted to show that the South, which had been pleading for peace and still stood on the defensive, had by this bombardment inaugurated a war against the United States. But it should be stated that the threats implied in the declarations that the Union could not exist part slave and part free, and that the Union should be preserved, and the denial of the right of a State peaceably to withdraw, were virtually a declaration of war, and the sending of an army and navy to attack was the result to have been anticipated as the consequence of such declaration of war."[135]

On the Confederacy's preparations for war:
☛ "At the North many had been deceived by the fictions of preparations at the South for the war of the sections, and among ourselves were few who realized how totally deficient the Southern States were in all which was necessary to the active operations of an army, however gallant the men might be, and however able were the generals who directed and led them. From these causes, operating jointly, resulted undue caution at the North and overweening confidence at the South."[136]

☛ "[Lincoln justified fomenting war on the South by saying] 'No choice was left but to call out the war power of the Government, and so to resist force employed for its destruction by force for its preservation.' . . . For what purpose must he call out this war power? He answers, by saying, 'and so to resist force employed for its destruction by force for its preservation.' But this which he asserts is not a fact. There was no 'force employed for its destruction.' Let the reader [bear in mind] the [many] fruitless efforts for peace which were made by us, and which Mr. Lincoln did not deign to notice. The assertion is not only incorrect, in stating that force was employed by us, but also in declaring that it was for the destruction of the Government of the United States. On the contrary, we wished to leave it alone. Our separation did not involve its destruction. To such fiction was Mr. Lincoln compelled to resort to give even apparent justice to his cause. He now goes to the Constitution for the exercise of his war power, and here we have another fiction."[137]

On the popular Yankee myth—still very much alive—that Southern black servants were little more than "abused livestock":
☛ "Among the less-informed persons at the North there exists an opinion that the negro slave at the South was a mere chattel, having neither rights nor immunities protected by law or public opinion. Southern men knew such was not the case, and others desiring to know could readily learn the fact. On that error the lauded story of *Uncle Tom's Cabin* was founded, but it is strange that a utilitarian and shrewd people did not ask why a slave, especially valuable, was the object of privation and abuse? Had it been a horse they would have been better able to judge, and would most probably have rejected the story for its improbability."[138]

On the commonly accepted Yankee myth that the South "attacked" the North at Fort Sumter:
☛ "[Based on the popular Northern fiction] . . . in regard to Fort Sumter, a child might suppose that a foreign army had attacked the United States—[and he] certainly could not learn that the State of South Carolina was merely seeking possession of a fort on her own soil, and claiming that her grant of the site had become void."[139]

8

THE CONFEDERACY

☛ ". . . the wish and policy of the [Confederate] government was peace."[140]

☛ "The tyranny of an unbridled majority, the most odious and the least responsible form of despotism, has denied us both the right and the remedy. Therefore, we are in arms to renew such sacrifices as our forefathers made to the holy cause of constitutional liberty."[141]

☛ "The declared compact of the Union from which we have withdrawn was to establish justice, ensure domestic tranquillity, provide for the common defence, promote the general welfare, and secure the blessings of liberty to ourselves and our posterity; and when in the judgment of the sovereign States now composing this confederacy, it has been perverted from the purposes for which it was ordained, and ceased to answer the ends for which it was established, a peaceful appeal to the ballot-box declared that, so far as they were concerned, the government created by that compact should cease to exist.

Davis' library at "Beauvoir."

In this they merely asserted the right which the Declaration of Independence of 1776 defined to be inalienable. Of the time and occasion of its exercise they as sovereigns were the final judges, each for itself."[142]

☛ "The impartial, enlightened verdict of mankind will vindicate the rectitude of our conduct; and He who knows the hearts of men will judge of the sincerity with which we labored to preserve the government of our fathers in its spirit."[143]

☛ "An agricultural people, whose chief interest is the export of commodities required in every manufacturing country, our true policy is peace, and the freest trade which our necessities will permit. It is alike our interest and that of all those to whom we would sell, and from whom we would buy, that there should be the fewest practicable restrictions upon the interchange of these commodities. There can, however, be but little rivalry between ours and any manufacturing or navigating community, such as the Northeastern States of the American Union. It must follow, therefore, that mutual interest will invite to good-will and kind offices on both parts. If, however, passion or lust of dominion should cloud the judgment or inflame the ambition of those States, we must prepare to meet the emergency and maintain, by the final arbitrament of the sword, the position which we have assumed among the nations of the earth."[144]

☛ "We have entered upon the career of independence, and it must be inflexibly pursued. Through many years of controversy with our late associates of the Northern States, we have vainly endeavored to secure tranquillity and obtain respect for the rights to which we were entitled. As a necessity, not a choice, we have resorted to the remedy of separation, and henceforth our energies must be directed to the conduct of our own affairs, and the perpetuity of the Confederacy which we have formed. If a just perception of mutual interest shall permit us peaceably to pursue our separate political career, my most earnest desire will have been fulfilled. But if this be denied to us, and the integrity of our territory and jurisdiction be assailed, it will but remain for us with firm resolve to appeal to arms and invoke the blessing of Providence on a just cause."[145]

☛ "The right solemnly proclaimed at the birth of the States, and which has been affirmed and reaffirmed in the bills of rights of the States subsequently admitted into the Union of 1789, undeniably recognizes in the people the power to resume the authority delegated for the purposes of government. Thus the sovereign States here represented, proceeded to form this [Southern] confederacy; and it is by the abuse of language that their act has been denominated 'revolution.' They formed a new alliance, but within each State its government has remained."[146]

☛ "Obstacles may retard, but they cannot long prevent the progress of a movement sanctified by its justice and sustained by a virtuous people."[147]

☛ "Actuated solely by the desire to preserve our own rights, and promote our own welfare, the separation by the Confederate States has been marked by no aggression upon others, and followed by no domestic convulsion."[148]

☛ "We have changed the constituent parts, but not the system of government. The Constitution framed by our fathers is that of these Confederate States. In their exposition of it, and in the judicial construction it has received, we have a light which reveals its true meaning. . . . Reverently let us invoke the God of our Fathers to guide and protect us in our efforts to perpetuate the principles which by his blessing they were able to vindicate, establish, and transmit to their posterity. With the continuance of his favor ever gratefully acknowledged, we may hopefully look forward to success, to peace, and to prosperity."[149]

On the loyalty of the men who became Confederate officers during the secession of the Southern states:
☛ ". . . against considerations of self-interest, and impelled by devotion to principle, they severed the ties, professional and personal, which had bound them [to the U.S.] from their youth up to the time when the Southern States, asserting the consecrated truth that all governments rest on the consent of the governed, decided to withdraw from the Union they had voluntarily entered, and the Northern States resolved to coerce them to remain in it against their will."[150]

☛ ". . . we must continue to struggle for our inherent right to freedom, independence, and self-government."[151]

☛ "I cannot believe that the cause for which our sacrifices were made can ever be lost, but rather hope that those who now deny the justice of our asserted claims will learn from experience that the fathers builded wisely and the Constitution should be construed according to the commentaries of the men who made it."[152]

9

THE CONFEDERATE CONSTITUTION

☞ "The supremacy of the states is the controlling idea."[153]

☞ "[In drawing up the Confederate Constitution the] Constitution of the United States was the model followed throughout, with only such changes as experience suggested for better practical working or for greater perspicuity. The preamble to both instruments is the same in substance, and very nearly identical in language. The words 'We, the people of the United States,' in one, are replaced by 'We, the people of the Confederate States,' in the other; and the gross perversion which has been made of the former expression is precluded in the latter merely by the addition of the explanatory clause, 'each State acting in its sovereign and independent character'—an explanation which, at the time of the formation of the Constitution of the United States, would have been deemed entirely superfluous."[154]

Davis' house at Richmond, Virginia.

☞ "The official term of the [Confederate] President was fixed at six instead of four years, and it was provided that he should not be eligible for reelection. This was in accordance with the original draft of the Constitution of 1787."[155]

☛ "Protective duties for the benefit of special branches of industry, which had been so fruitful a source of trouble under the Government of the United States, were altogether prohibited [in the Confederate Constitution]. So, also, were bounties from the Treasury, and extra compensation for services rendered by officers, contractors, or employees, of any description."[156]

☛ "A vote of two thirds of each House was requisite for the appropriation of money from the Treasury, unless asked for by the chief of a department and submitted to Congress by the President, or for payment of the expenses of Congress, or of claims against the Confederacy judicially established and declared. The President was also authorized to approve any one appropriation and disapprove any other in the same bill."[157]

☛ "With regard to slavery and the slave-trade, the provisions of this Constitution furnish an effectual answer to the assertion, so often made, that the Confederacy was founded on slavery, that slavery was its 'corner-stone,' etc. Property in slaves, already existing, was recognized and guaranteed, just as it was by the Constitution of the United States; and the rights of such property in the common Territories were protected against any such hostile discrimination as had been attempted in the Union. But the 'extension of slavery,' in the only practical sense of that phrase, was more distinctly and effectually precluded by the Confederate than by the Federal Constitution. This will be manifest on a comparison of the provisions of the two relative to the slave-trade. These are found at the beginning of the ninth section of the first article of each instrument.

"The Constitution of the United States has the following: 'The migration or importation of such persons as any of the States now existing shall think proper to admit, shall not be prohibited by the Congress prior to the year one thousand eight hundred and eight; but a tax or duty may be imposed on such importations, not exceeding ten dollars for each person.'

"The Confederate Constitution, on the other hand, ordained as follows: '1. The importation of negroes of the African race from any foreign country, other than the slaveholding States or Territories of the United States of America, is hereby forbidden; and Congress is required to pass such laws as shall effectually prevent the same. 2. Congress shall also have the power to prohibit the introduction of slaves from any State not a member of, or Territory not belonging to, this Confederacy.'"[158]

☛ "In the case of the United States, the only prohibition is against any interference by Congress with the slave-trade for a term of years, and it was further legitimized by the authority given to impose a duty upon it. The term of years, it is true, had long since expired, but there was still no prohibition of the trade by the [U.S.] Constitution; it was after 1808 entirely within the discretion of Congress either to encourage, tolerate, or prohibit it.

"Under the Confederate Constitution, on the contrary, the African slave-trade was 'hereby forbidden' positively and unconditionally, from the beginning. Neither the Confederate Government nor that of any of the States could permit it, and the Congress was expressly 'required' to enforce the prohibition. The only discretion in the matter intrusted to the Congress was, whether or not to permit the introduction of slaves from any of the United States or their Territories."[159]

☛ "Mr. Lincoln, in his inaugural address, had said: 'I have no purpose, directly or indirectly, to interfere with the institution of slavery in the States where it exists. I believe I have no lawful right to do so, and I have no inclination to do so.' Now, if there was no purpose on the part of the Government of the United States to interfere with the institution of slavery within its already existing limits—a proposition which permitted its propagation within those limits by natural increase—and inasmuch as the Confederate Constitution precluded any other than the same natural increase, we may plainly perceive the disingenuousness and absurdity of the pretension by which a factitious sympathy has been obtained in certain quarters for the war upon the South, on the ground that it was a war in behalf of freedom against slavery."[160]

On the importance of the new Confederate Constitution:
☛ "We are fighting for Constitutional liberty; upon us depends its last hope. The Yankees, in endeavoring to coerce the States, have lost that heir-loom of their fathers, and the men of the South alone must sustain it.

"Ours is not a revolution. We are a free and independent people in States that had the right to make a better Government when they saw fit. [The North] . . . sought to infringe upon the rights we had, and we only instituted a new Government on the basis of these rights."[161]

To those who attempted to trivialize the formation of the Confederacy:
☛ "For proof of the sincerity of our purpose to maintain our ancient institutions, we may point to the Constitution of the Confederacy and the laws enacted under it, as well as to the fact that through all the necessities of an unequal struggle there has been [unlike Lincoln and the Yankee government] no act on our part to impair personal liberty or the freedom of speech, of thought, or of the press."[162]

On the reason for creating a new Confederacy and constitution:
☛ "The main, if not the only, purpose for which independent states form unions, or confederations, is to combine the power of the several members in such manner as to form one united force in all relations with foreign powers, whether in peace or in war. Each state, amply competent to administer and control its own domestic government, yet too feeble successfully to resist powerful nations, seeks safety by uniting with other states in like condition, and by delegating to some common agent the use of the combined strength of all, in order to secure advantageous commercial relations in peace, and to carry on hostilities with effect in war."[163]

☛ "I had no direct part in the preparation of the Confederate Constitution. No consideration of delicacy forbids me, therefore, to say . . . that it was a model of wise, temperate, and liberal statesmanship. Intelligent criticism, from hostile as well as friendly sources, has been compelled to admit its excellences, and has sustained the judgment of a popular Northern journal which said, a few days after it was adopted and published: 'The new [Confederate] Constitution is the Constitution of the United States with various modifications and some very important and most desirable improvements. We are free to say that the invaluable reforms enumerated should be adopted by the United States, with or without a reunion of the seceded States, and as soon as possible. But why not accept them with the propositions of the Confederate States on slavery as a basis of reunion?'"[164]

10

THE

CONFEDERATE PRESIDENCY

☛ "I will devote to the duties of the high office to which I have been called all I have of heart, of head and of hand."[165]

☛ ". . . I enter upon the duties of the office [of president] to which I have been chosen with the hope that the beginning of our career, as a Confederacy, may not be obstructed by hostile opposition to our enjoyment of the separate existence and independence we have asserted, and which, with the blessing of Providence, we intend to maintain."[166]

Another view of Davis at "Beauvoir."

☛ "It will not be amiss here briefly to state what were my position and feelings at the period now under consideration, as they have been the subject of gross and widespread misrepresentation. It is not only untrue, but absurd, to attribute to me motives of personal ambition to be gratified by a dismemberment of the Union. Much of my life had been spent in the military and civil service of the United States. Whatever reputation I had acquired was identified with their history; and, if future preferment had been the object, it would have led me to cling to the Union as long as a shred of it should remain. If any, judging after the event, should assume that I was allured by the high office subsequently conferred upon me by the people of the Confederate States, the answer to any such conclusion has been made by others, to whom it was well known, before the Confederacy was formed, that I had no desire to be its President. When the suggestion was made to me, I expressed a decided objection, and gave reasons of a public and permanent character against being placed in that position."[167]

☛ "Furthermore, I then held the office of United States Senator from Mississippi—one which I preferred to all others. The kindness of the people had three times conferred it upon me, and I had no reason to fear that it would not be given again, as often as desired. So far from wishing to change this position for any other, I had specially requested my friends (some of whom had thought of putting me in nomination for the Presidency of the United States in 1860) not to permit 'my name to be used before the Convention for any nomination whatever.'"[168]

To his Southern constituents toward the end of Lincoln's War:
☛ "Animated by the confidence in your spirit and fortitude, which never yet has failed me, I announce to you, fellow-countrymen, that it is my purpose to maintain your cause with my whole heart and soul; that I will never consent to abandon to the enemy one foot of the soil of any one of the States of the Confederacy . . ."[169]

To his Southern constituents after Lincoln's War:
☛ "I stand before you . . . a man without a country, for my ambition lies buried in the grave of the Confederacy. . . . [Nonetheless, the] past is dead; let it bury its dead, its hopes and its aspirations. Before you lies the future—a future full of golden promise, a future full of recompense for honorable endeavor, a future of expanding national glory, before which all the world shall stand amazed. Let me beseech you to lay aside all rancor, all bitter sectional feeling, and to take your places in the ranks of those who will bring about a consummation devoutly to be wished—a reunited country."[170]

11

SLAVERY & BLACKS

☛ "African servitude [in the South was] . . . confessedly the mildest and most humane of all institutions to which the name 'slavery' has ever been applied . . ."[171]

On the existence of indigenous African slavery, which preceded American slavery by millennia:

☛ "The forefathers of . . . [Southern black servants] were gathered from the torrid plains and malarial swamps of inhospitable Africa. Generally they were born [there as] the slaves of barbarian masters, untaught in all the useful arts and occupations, reared in heathen darkness, and, sold by heathen masters, they were transferred to shores enlightened by the rays of Christianity."[172]

Brierfield, Davis' plantation home during his early adult years. Originally located about twenty miles south of Vicksburg, Mississippi, on what is now Davis Island, it burned down in 1931.

☛ "When at a subsequent period there arose in the Northern States an antislavery agitation [about 1830], it was a harmless and scarcely noticed movement until political demagogues seized upon it as a means to acquire power. Had it been left to pseudo-philanthropists and fanatics, most zealous where least informed, it never could have shaken the foundations of the Union and have incited one section to carry fire and sword into the other."[173]

☛ "The Southern States have been persistently represented as the propagandists of slavery, and the Northern States as the defenders and champions of universal freedom. It has been dogmatically asserted that the war between the States was caused by efforts on the one side to extend and perpetuate human slavery, and on the other to resist it and establish human liberty. Neither allegation is true. To whatever extent the question of slavery may have served as an occasion, it was far from being the cause of the war."[174]

☛ "As an historical fact, negro slavery existed in all the original thirteen States. It was recognized by the Constitution. Owing to climatic, industrial, and economical—not moral or sentimental—reasons, it had gradually disappeared in the Northern States, while it had persisted in the Southern States. The slave-trade was never conducted by the people of the South. It had been monopolized by Northern merchants and carried on in Northern ships. Men differed in their views as to the abstract question of the right or wrong of slavery; but, for two generations after the [American] Revolution, there was no geographical line of such differences. It was during the controversy over the Missouri question [in 1820] that the subject first took a sectional aspect; but long after that period Abolitionists were mobbed and assaulted in the North. [Yankee abolitionist Elijah P.] Lovejoy, for example, was killed in Illinois in 1837."[175]

☛ "Compare the slaves in the Southern States with recently imported Africans as seen in the West Indies, and who can fail to be struck with the increased improvement of the race; whether physically, morally, or intellectually considered? Compare our slaves with the free blacks of the Northern States, and you will find the one contented, well provided for in all their physical wants, and steadily improving in their moral condition; the other miserable, impoverished, loathsome for the deformity and disease which follow after penury and vice, covering the records of the criminal courts, and filling the penitentiaries. Mark the [Northern] hostility to caste, the social degradation which excludes the able from employment of profit and trust, and leaves the helpless to want and neglect. Then turn to the condition of this race in the States of the South, and view them in the relation of slaves. There, no hostility exists against them—the master is the natural protector of his slave; and public opinion, common feeling, mere interest would not allow him to neglect his wants."[176]

☛ "Slavery never was an essential element in the War. It was only a means of bringing other conflicting elements to an earlier culmination. It fired the musket which was already capped and loaded."[177]

On the age-old universality of slavery:

☛ "[It is a fact that slavery] was established by decree of Almighty God, that it is sanctioned in the Bible, in both Testaments, from Genesis to Revelations; that it has existed in all ages; has been found among the people of the highest civilization, and in nations of the highest proficiency in the arts."[178]

☛ "Slavery existed then in the earliest ages, and among the chosen people of God; and in Revelation we are told that it shall exist till the end of time shall come. You find it in the Old and in the New Testament—in the prophecies, psalms, and the epistles of Paul; you find it recognized—sanctioned everywhere. It is the Bible and the Constitution on which we rely, and we are not to be answered by the dicta of earthly wisdom, or more earthly arrogance, when we have these high authorities to teach and to construe the decrees of God."[179]

☛ "The African slave trade was carried on almost exclusively by New England merchants and Northern ships."[180]

☛ "It is well known that, at the time of the adoption of the Federal Constitution, African servitude existed in all the States that were parties to that compact, unless with the single exception of Massachusetts [which gave birth to the American slave trade in 1638], in which it had, perhaps, very recently ceased to exist. The slaves, however, were numerous in the Southern, and very few in the Northern, States. This diversity was occasioned by differences of climate, soil, and industrial interests—not in any degree by moral considerations, which at that period were not recognized as an element in the question. It was simply because negro labor was more profitable in the South than in the North that the importation of negro slaves had been, and continued to be, chiefly directed to the Southern ports. For the same reason slavery was abolished by the States of the Northern section (though it existed in several of them for more than fifty years after the adoption of the Constitution), while the importation of slaves into the South continued to be carried on by Northern merchants and Northern ships, without interference in the traffic from any quarter, until it was prohibited by the spontaneous action of the Southern States themselves [in early 1861, under the Confederate Constitution]."[181]

☛ "The reader of many of the treatises on these events, which have been put forth as historical, if dependent upon such alone for information, might naturally enough be led to the conclusion that the controversies which arose between the States, and the war in which they culminated, were caused by efforts on the one side to extend and perpetuate human slavery, and on the other to resist it and establish human liberty. The Southern States and Southern people have been sedulously represented as 'propagandists' of slavery, and the Northern as the defenders and champions of universal freedom, and this view has been so arrogantly assumed, so dogmatically asserted, and so persistently reiterated, that its authors have, in many cases, perhaps, succeeded in bringing themselves to believe it, as well as in impressing it widely upon the world."[182]

☛ "The [U.S.] Constitution expressly forbade any interference by Congress with the slave-trade—or, to use its own language, with the 'migration or importation of such persons' as any of the States should think proper to admit—'prior to the year 1808.' During the intervening period of more than twenty years, the matter was exclusively under the control of the respective States. Nevertheless, every Southern State, without exception, either had already enacted, or proceeded to enact, laws forbidding the importation of slaves. Virginia was the first of all the States, North or South, to prohibit it, and Georgia was the first to incorporate such a prohibition in her organic Constitution."[183]

☛ "Much of . . . [the Confederacy's] success was due to the much-abused institution of African servitude, for it enabled the white men to go into the army, and leave the cultivation of their fields and the care of their flocks, as well as of their wives and children, to those who, in the language of the Constitution, were 'held to service or labor.' A passing remark may here be appropriate as to the answer thus afforded to the clamor about the 'horrors of slavery.'

"Had these Africans been a cruelly oppressed people, restlessly struggling to be freed from their bonds, would their masters have dared to leave them, as was done, and would they have remained as they did, continuing their usual duties, or could the proclamation of emancipation have been put on the plea of a military necessity, if the fact had been that the negroes were forced to serve, and desired only an opportunity to rise against their masters? It will be remembered that, when the proclamation was issued, it was confessed by President Lincoln to be a nullity beyond the limit within which it could be enforced by the Federal troops."[184]

On the enlistment of Southern black servants into the Confederate army and navy, and their subsequent emancipation:
☞ "Viewed merely as property, and therefore as the subject of impressment, the service or labor of the slave has been frequently claimed for short periods in the construction of defensive works. The slave, however, bears another relation to the state—that of a person. . . . The policy of engaging to liberate the negro on his discharge after service faithfully rendered seems to me preferable to that of granting immediate manumission, or that of retaining him in servitude."[185]

To a Yank:
☞ "And for what end, sir, is all this aggression? They see that the slaves in their present condition in the South are comfortable and happy; they see them advancing in intelligence; they see the kindest relations existing between them and their masters; they see them provided for in age and sickness, in infancy and in disability; they see them in useful employment, restrained from the vicious indulgences to which their inferior nature [that is, their archaic African hunting and gathering lifestyle] inclines them; they see our penitentiaries never filled, and our poor-houses usually empty. Let them turn to the other hand, and they see the same race in a state of freedom at the North; but, instead of the comfort and kindness they receive at the South, instead of being happy and useful, they are, with few exceptions, miserable, degraded, filling the penitentiaries and poor-houses, objects of scorn, excluded in some places from the schools, and deprived of many other privileges and benefits which attach to the white men among whom they live. And yet they insist that elsewhere an institution which has proved beneficial to this race shall be abolished, that it may be substituted by a state of things which is fraught with so many evils to the race which they claim to be the object of their solicitude!"[186]

12

ABRAHAM LINCOLN

☛ "The man was nothing, save as he was the representative of opinions, of a policy, of purposes, of power, to inflict upon us those wrongs to which freemen never tamely submit."[187]

☛ "The indignation with which the result of the [1860] Presidential election was received in the Southern States proceeded from no personal hostility to the President-elect, nor from chagrin at the defeat of the Democratic candidates, but from the fact that the people of the South recognized in Mr. Lincoln the representative of a party professing principles destructive to 'their peace, their prosperity, and their domestic tranquillity.'"[188]

☛ "[On April 15, 1861] President Lincoln, introducing his farce 'of combinations too powerful to be suppressed by the ordinary course of judicial proceedings,' called forth the military of the several States to the number of seventy-five thousand, and commanded 'the persons composing the combinations' to disperse, etc. It can but surprise any one in the least degree conversant with the history of the Union, to find States referred to as 'persons composing combinations,' and that the sovereign creators of the Federal Government, the States of the Union, should be commanded by their agent to disperse. The levy of so large an army could only mean war; but the power to declare war did not reside in the President—it was delegated to the Congress only. If, however, it had been a riotous combination or an insurrection, it must have been, according to the Constitution, against the State; and the power

Abraham Lincoln, big government, Constitution-loathing Liberal; arch nemesis of Davis, small government, Constitution-loving conservative.

of the President to call forth the militia to suppress it, was dependent upon an application from the State for that purpose; it could not precede such application, and still less could it be rightfully exercised against the will of a State. . . . In any possible view of the case, therefore, the conclusion must be, that the calling on some of the States for seventy-five thousand militia to invade other States which were asserted to be still in the Union, was a palpable violation of the Constitution, and the usurpation of undelegated power, or, in other words, of power reserved to the States or to the people."[189]

☛ "[Lincoln took] rapid strides toward despotism made under the mask of preserving the Union. Yet these and similar measures were tolerated because the sectional hate dominated in the Northern states over the higher motives of constitutional and moral obligation."[190]

On Lincoln's war crimes:
☛ "Thenceforward, arrests of the most illustrious became the rule. In a land where freedom of speech was held to be an unquestioned right, freedom of thought ceased to exist, and men were incarcerated for opinion's sake. . . . But this was only the beginning of unbridled despotism and a reign of terror."[191]

☛ "It was an artful scheme to awaken a controversy in the slave States, and to commence the work of emancipation by holding out pecuniary aid as an inducement. In every previous declaration the President had said that he did not contemplate any interference with domestic slavery within the States. The resolution was passed by large majorities in each House.

"This proposition of President Lincoln was wholly unconstitutional, because it attempted to do what was expressly forbidden by the Constitution. It proposed a contract between the State of Missouri and the Government of the United States which, in the language of the act, shall be 'irrepealable without the consent of the United States.' The words of the Constitution are as follows: 'No State shall enter into any treaty, alliance, or confederation, grant letters of marque and reprisal, coin money, etc.'

"This is a prohibition not only upon the power of one State to enter into a compact, alliance, confederation, or agreement with another State, but also with the Government of the United States.

". . . this measure was to be consummated under the war power; that whatever was necessary to carry on the war to a successful conclusion might be done without restraint under the authority, not of the Constitution, but as a military necessity."[192]

☞ ". . . it should be remembered that, if the necessity which they pleaded was an argument to justify their violations of all the provisions of the Constitution, the existence of such a necessity on their part was a sufficient argument to justify our withdrawal from union with them. If necessity on their part justified a violation of the Constitution, necessity on our part justified secession from them. If the preservation of the existence of the Union by coercion of the States was an argument to justify these violent usurpations by the United States Government, it was still more forcibly an argument to justify our separation and resistance to invasion; for we were struggling for our natural rights, but the Government of the United States has no natural rights."[193]

☞ "On January 1, 1863, another proclamation was issued by the President of the United States declaring the emancipation to be absolute within the Confederate States, with the exception of a few districts [that were under Yankee control]. The closing words of the proclamation were these: 'And upon this act, sincerely believed to be an act of justice, warranted by the Constitution upon military necessity, I invoke the considerate judgment of mankind and the gracious favor of Almighty God.'

"Let us test the existence of the military necessity here spoken of by a few facts. The white male population of the Northern States was then 13,690,364. The white male population of the Confederate States was 5,449,463. The number of troops which the United States had called into the field exceeded one million men. The number of troops which the Confederate Government had then in the field was less than four hundred thousand men. The United States Government had a navy which was only third in rank in the world. The Confederate Government had a navy which at that time consisted of a single small ship on the ocean. The people of the United States had a commerce afloat all over the world. The people of the Confederate States had not a single port open to commerce. The people of the United States were the rivals of the greatest nations in all kinds of manufactures. The people of the Confederate States had few manufactures, and those were of articles of inferior importance. The Government of the United States possessed the Treasury of a Union of eighty years with its vast resources. The Confederate States had to create a Treasury by the development of financial resources. The ambassadors and representatives of the former were welcomed at every court in the world. The representatives of the latter were not recognized anywhere."[194]

On Lincoln's well-known lifelong black colonization campaign to emancipate Southern slaves so he could "ship them back to Africa," as he put it in a public speech on August 21, 1858:
☛ "The President of the United States, in his message of December 3, 1861, stated that numbers of persons held to service [that is, 'slaves'] had been liberated and were dependent on the United States, and must be provided for in some way. He recommended that steps be taken for colonizing them at some places in a climate congenial to them."[195]

☛ "[Regarding our true constitutional principles,] the President of the United States perverted them, misstated them, and sought to reach his ends by groundless fabrications—as if he would enforce a fiction or establish a fallacy to be as good as truth. It might be still further shown, if it had not already become self-evident, that this method was pursued with such a perversity and wickedness as to render it a characteristic feature of that war administration on whose skirts is the blood of more than a million of human beings."[196]

☛ "Who shall decide? Which is sovereign, Mr. Lincoln and his proclamation or the Constitution? The Constitution says: 'This Constitution, and the laws of the United States which shall be made in pursuance thereof, shall be the supreme law of the land.' Was it thus obeyed by Mr. Lincoln as the supreme law of the land? It was not obeyed, but set aside, subverted, overturned by him. But he said in his oath: 'I do solemnly swear that I will, to the best of my ability, preserve, protect, and defend the Constitution of the United States.'

"Did he do it? Is such treatment of the Constitution the manner to preserve, protect, and defend it? Of what value, then, are paper constitutions and oaths binding officers to their preservation, if there is not intelligence enough in the people to discern the violations, and virtue enough to resist the violators?"[197]

On Lincoln's war against the U.S. Constitution:
☛ "It is amazing to see the utter forgetfulness of all constitutional obligations and the entire disregard of the conditions of the laws of nations . . . [by] the President of the United States. Was he ignorant of their

existence, or did he seek to cover up his violation of them by a deceptive use of language? . . . Let posterity answer the questions: Who were the revolutionists? Who were really destroying the Constitution of the United States?"[198]

To his Confederate soldiers on their fight against Lincoln and his invaders:
☛ ". . . you have a cause which binds you together more firmly than your [Revolutionary War] fathers were. They fought to be free from the usurpation of the British crown; but they fought against a manly foe. You fight the offscourings [that is, rubbish and refuse] of the earth."[199]

☛ "The tyrant's plea of necessity to excuse despotic usurpation is offered for the unconstitutional act of emancipation, and the poor resort to prejudice is invoked in the use of the epithet 'rebellion'—a word inapplicable to States generally, and most especially so to the sovereign members of a voluntary union. But, alas for their ancient prestige, they have even lost the plural reference they had in the Constitution, and seem so small to this utilizing tuition as to be described by the neutral pronoun 'it!' Such language would be appropriate to an imperial Government, which in absorbing territories required the subjected inhabitants to swear allegiance to it."[200]

On the April 15, 1865, news that Lincoln had been killed by an assassin's bullet:
☛ "Some troopers encamped in the vicinity had collected to see me; they called to the gentleman who had the dispatch in his hand, no doubt supposing it to be army news. He complied with their request [to read it aloud], and a few . . . cheered, as was natural at news of the fall of one they considered their most powerful foe.

"For an enemy so relentless in the war for our subjugation, we could not be expected to mourn . . ."[201]

13

LINCOLN'S WAR

On the South's reason for going to war with the North:
☞ "The object was to sustain a principle—the broad principle of constitutional liberty, the right of self-government."[202]

On the North's reason for going to war with the South:
☞ ". . . to establish the supremacy of the General Government on the ruins of the blood-bought independence of the States."[203]

☞ ". . . when the aim of the aggressor is 'power, plunder, and extended rule'—there will be no concessions by him, no compromises, no adjustment of results. The alternative is subjugation by the sword, or peace by absolute submission. The latter condition could not be accepted by us. The former was, therefore, to be resisted as best we might."[204]

Conservative Davis and the Confederate army fought to preserve the Constitution and its tacit guarantee of states' rights (as embodied in the Tenth Amendment). Liberal Lincoln and the Union army fought to destroy it.

☞ "The attempt to represent us as the aggressors in the conflict which ensued is as unfounded as the complaint made by the wolf against the lamb in the familiar tale. He who makes the assault is not necessarily he that strikes the first blow or fires the first gun."[205]

☞ "[The Lincoln] Government dare not go before the people with a plain avowal of its real purposes and of their consequences. No, sir; the policy is to inveigle the people of the North into civil war, by masking the design in smooth and ambiguous terms."[206]

☞ "[The antiwar ideas expressed by those Yankees who preferred to let the South go in peace] were so entirely swept away by the tide of reckless fury which soon afterward impelled an armed invasion of the South, that (with a few praiseworthy but powerless exceptions) scarcely a vestige of them was left. Not only were they obliterated, but seemingly forgotten. . . . [It is apparent that] in times of revolutionary excitement, the higher and better elements are crushed and silenced by the lower and baser—not so much on account of their greater extent, as of their greater violence."[207]

☞ "To preserve a sectional equilibrium and to maintain the equality of the States was the effort on one side, to acquire empire was the manifest purpose on the other. This struggle began before the men of the Confederacy were born . . ."[208]

☞ ". . . military preparations were pushed forward [in the North] for the unconstitutional, criminal purpose of coercing States . . ."[209]

☞ "[At the beginning of 1862 the U.S. Congress] had no sooner assembled than it brought forward the doctrine that the Government of the United States was engaged in a struggle for its existence, and could therefore resort to any measure which a case of self-defense would justify. It pretended not to know that the only self-defense authorized in the Constitution for the Government created by it, was by the peaceful method of the ballot-box; and that, so long as the Government fulfilled the objects of its creation (see preamble of the Constitution), and exercised its delegated powers within their prescribed limits, its surest and strongest defense was to be found in that ballot-box."[210]

☞ "The Congress next declared that our institution of slavery was the cause of all the troubles of the country, and therefore the whole power of the Government must be so directed as to remove it. If this had really been the cause of the troubles, how easily wise and patriotic statesmen might have furnished a relief. Nearly all the slaveholding States had withdrawn from the Union, therefore those [Northern ones] who had been suffering vicariously might have welcomed their departure, as the removal of the cause which disturbed the Union, and have tried the experiment of separation. Should the trial have brought more wisdom and a spirit of conciliation to either or both, there might have arisen, as a result of the experiment, a reconstructed fraternal Union such as our fathers designed."[211]

☛ "For a State or union of States to attack with military force another State, is to make war. By the Constitution, the power to make war is given solely to Congress. 'Congress shall have power to declare war,' says the Constitution. . . . Thus, under a perverted use of language, the Executive at Washington [that is, Lincoln] did that which he undeniably had no power to do . . . [and] early was commenced a long series of usurpations of powers inconsistent with the purposes for which the Union was formed, and destructive of the fraternity it was designed to perpetuate."[212]

☛ "The issue before us is one of no ordinary character. We are not engaged in a conflict for conquest or for aggrandizement, or for the settlement of a point of international law. The question for you to decide is: 'Will you be slaves or will you be independent?' Will you transmit to your children the freedom and equality which your fathers transmitted to you, or will you bow down in adoration before an idol baser than ever was worshipped by Eastern idolaters?"[213]

☛ "A question settled by violence, or in disregard of law, must remain unsettled forever."[214]

☛ "Those [Northern] men who now assail us, who have been associated with us in a common union, who have inherited a government which they claim to be the best the world ever saw—these men, when left to themselves, have shown that they are incapable of preserving their own personal liberty. They have destroyed the freedom of the press; they have seized upon and imprisoned members of State Legislatures and of municipal councils, who were suspected of sympathy with the South; men have been carried off into captivity in distant States without indictment, without a knowledge of the accusations brought against them, in utter defiance of all rights guaranteed by the institutions under which they live. These people, when separated from the South and left entirely to themselves, have, in six months, demonstrated their utter incapacity for self government. And yet, these are the people who claim to be your masters. These are the people who have determined to divide out the South among their Federal troops. Mississippi they have devoted to the direst vengeance of all. 'But vengeance is the Lord's,' and beneath his banner you will meet and hurl back these worse than vandal hordes."[215]

☛ "The [Northern] authors of the aggressions which had disturbed the harmony of the Union had lately acquired power on a sectional basis, and were eager for the spoil of their sectional victory. To conceal their real motive, and artfully to appeal to the prejudice of foreigners, they declared that slavery was the cause of the troubles of the country, and of the 'rebellion' which they were engaged in suppressing. In his inaugural address in March, 1861, President Lincoln said: 'I have no purpose, directly or indirectly, to interfere with the institution of slavery in the States where it exists. I believe I have no lawful right to do so, and I have no inclination to do so.' The leader [Charles Sumner of Massachusetts] of the Abolition party in Congress, on February 25, 1861, said in the Senate, 'I take this occasion to declare most explicitly that I do not think that Congress has any right to interfere with slavery in a State.' The principle thus announced had regulated all the legislation of Congress from the beginning of its first session in 1789 down to the first session of the Thirty-seventh Congress, commencing July 4, 1861.

"A few months after the inaugural address above cited and the announcement of the fact above quoted were made, [the U.S.] Congress commenced to legislate for the abolition of slavery. If it had the power now to do what it before had not, whence was it derived? There had been no addition in the interval to the grants in the Constitution; not a word or letter of that instrument had been changed since the possession of the power was disclaimed; yet after July 4, 1861, it was asserted by the majority in [the U.S.] Congress that the [Lincoln] Government had power to interfere with slavery in the States. Whence came the change? The answer is, It was wrought by the same process and on the same plea that tyranny has ever employed against liberty and justice—the time-worn excuse of usurpers—*necessity*; an excuse which is ever assumed as valid, because the usurper claims to be the sole judge of his necessity."[216]

On hearing that Lincoln would consider offering the seceded Southern states "compensated emancipation, no confiscation [of slaves], and amnesty," if they would return to the Union:

☛ ". . . amnesty, sir, applies to criminals. We have committed no crime. Confiscation is of no account unless you can enforce it; and emancipation! you have already emancipated nearly two millions of our slaves, and if you will take care of them you may emancipate the rest. I had a few when the war began. I was of some use to them; they never were of any to me. Against their will you emancipated them; and you may emancipate every negro in the Confederacy; but we will be free! We will govern ourselves! We will do it, if we have to see every Southern plantation sacked, and every Southern city in flames."[217]

☛ "I once loved the old [U.S.] flag as well as you [Yanks] do. I would have died for it; but now it is to me only the emblem of oppression."[218]

☛ "Rapine and wanton destruction of private property, war upon non-combatants, murder of captives, bloody threats to avenge the death of an invading soldiery by the slaughter of unarmed citizens, orders of banishment against peaceful farmers engaged in the cultivation of the soil, are some of the means used by our ruthless invaders to enforce the submission of a free people to a foreign sway."[219]

☛ ". . . whatever of bloodshed, of devastation, or shock to republican government has resulted from the war, is to be charged to the Northern States. The invasions of the Southern States, for purposes of coercion, were in violation of the written Constitution, and the attempt to subjugate sovereign States, under the pretext of 'preserving the Union,' was alike offensive to law, to good morals, and the proper use of language. The Union was the voluntary junction of free and independent States; to subjugate any of them was to destroy constituent parts, and necessarily, therefore, must be the destruction of the Union itself."[220]

☛ "[Just prior to the War, warmongering Northern politicians exhibited alarm] at the prospect of compromise and a concurrent change of opinion. [They then urged] the sending of 'stiff-backed' men, to thwart the threatened success of the friends of peace, and [concluded] with an expression of the humane and patriotic sentiment that 'without a little bloodletting' the Union would not be 'worth a rush.' With such unworthy levity did these leaders of sectional strife express their exultation in the prospect of the conflict, which was to drench the land with blood and enshroud thousands of homes in mourning!"[221]

When asked by a Northerner how the War could be stopped:
☛ "In a very simple way. Withdraw your armies from our territory, and

peace will come of itself. We do not seek to subjugate you. We are not waging an offensive war, except so far as it is offensive-defensive,—that is, so far as we are forced to invade you, to prevent your invading us. Let us alone, and peace will come at once. . . . You would deny to us what you exact for yourselves,—the right of self-government."[222]

On the effort of Southern politicians, prior to Lincoln's War, to try and avoid bloodshed in the face of the North's ominous threats of invasion and violence:
☛ ". . . if we could have foreseen the ultimate failure of all efforts for a peaceful settlement, and the [Yankee] perfidy that was afterward to be practiced in connection with them, our advice would have been different."[223]

To a Yank:
☛ "You have sown such bitterness at the South; you have put such an ocean of blood between the two countries, that I despair of seeing any harmony in my time. Our children may forget this war, but we cannot."[224]

☛ "I tried all in my power to avert this war. I saw it coming, and for twelve years I worked night and day to prevent it; but I could not. The North was mad and blind; it would not let us govern ourselves, and so the war came, and now it must go on till the last man of this generation falls in his tracks, and his children seize his musket and fight our battle, unless you acknowledge our right to self-government. We are not fighting for slavery. We are fighting for independence, and that, or extermination, we will have."[225]

On the barbarities of Union General William T. Sherman at Atlanta, Georgia:
☛ "General Sherman, desisting from any further aggressive movement in the field, returned to Atlanta, which had been formally surrendered by the Mayor on September 2d, with the promise, as reported, on the part of the Federal commander, that non-combatants and private property should be respected. Shortly after his arrival, the commanding General of the Federal forces, forgetful of this promise, and on the pretense that the exigencies of the service required that the place should be used exclusively for military purposes, issued an order directing all civilians living in Atlanta, male and female, to leave the city within five days from the date of the order (September 5th). Since Alva's atrocious cruelties to the non-combatant population of the Low Countries in the sixteenth century, the history of war records no instance of such barbarous cruelty as that which this order

designed to perpetrate. It involved the immediate expulsion from their homes and only means of subsistence of thousands of unoffending women and children, whose husbands and fathers were either in the army, in Northern prisons, or had died in battle. In vain did the Mayor and corporate authorities of Atlanta appeal to Sherman to revoke or modify this inhuman order, representing in piteous language 'the woe, the horror, and the suffering, not to be described by words,' which its execution would inflict on helpless women and infant children. His only reply was: 'I give full credit to your statements of the distress that will be occasioned by it, and yet shall not revoke my order, because my orders are not designed to meet the humanities of the case.'

"At the time appointed, the women and children were expelled from their houses, and, before they were passed within our lines, complaint was generally made that the Federal officers and men who were sent to guard them had robbed them of the few articles of value they had been permitted to take from their homes. The cowardly dishonesty of its executioners was in perfect harmony with the temper and spirit of the order. . . . [The] line of his march could be traced by the burning dwelling houses and by the wail of women and children pitilessly left to die from starvation and exposure in the depth of winter . . ."[226]

☛ "Lee had never contemplated surrender. He had, long before, in language similar to that employed by [George] Washington during the Revolution, expressed to me the belief that in the mountains of Virginia he could carry on the war for twenty years . . ."[227]

☛ "The war, which in its inception was waged for forcing us back into the Union, having failed in accomplishing that purpose, passed into a second stage, in which it was attempted to conquer and rule our States as dependent provinces. Defeated in this design, our adversaries entered upon another, which could have no other purpose than revenge and plunder of private property. In May, 1864, it was still characterized by the barbarism with which it had been previously conducted. Aged men, helpless women and children, appealed in vain to the humanity which should be inspired by their condition, for immunity from arrest, incarceration, or banishment from their homes. Plunder and devastation of the property of non-combatants, destruction of private dwellings, and even of edifices devoted to the worship of God; expeditions organized for the sole purpose of sacking cities, consigning them to the flames, killing the unarmed inhabitants, and inflicting horrible outrages on women and children, were some of the constantly recurring atrocities of the [Yankee] invader."[228]

On Union General William T. Sherman's crimes during his infamous "March to the Sea" (Nov. 15-Dec. 21, 1864):
☞ "[Sherman] resolved upon his march to the sea, abandoning Atlanta, after having first utterly destroyed that city by fire. Not a single house was spared, not even a church. Similar acts of vandalism marked the progress of the Federal army at Rome, Kingston, Acworth, Marietta, and every town or village along its route, thus carrying out General Sherman's order 'to enforce a devastation more or less relentless' along the line of his march, where he only encountered helpless women and children. The arson of the dwelling-houses of non-combatants and the robbery of their property, extending even to the trinkets worn by women, made the devastation as relentless as savage instincts could suggest."[229]

Speaking to his fellow Southerners:
☞ ". . . if we were without money, without food, without weapons,—if our whole country were desolated, and our armies crushed and disbanded,—could we, without giving up our manhood, give up our right to govern ourselves? Would you not rather die, and feel yourself a man, than live, and be subject to a foreign power?"[230]

☞ "Those who are to come after us, and who will look without prejudice or excitement at the record of events that occurred in our day, will not fail to wonder how [those in the North] . . . should have so far imposed on the credulity of the world as to be able to arrogate to themselves the claim of being the special friends of a Union, contracted in order to 'insure domestic tranquillity' among the people of the States united; that they were the advocates of peace, of law, and of order, who, when taking an oath to support and maintain the Constitution, did so with a mental reservation to violate one of the provisions of that Constitution—one of the conditions of the compact without which the Union could never have been formed."[231]

To a Yank during Lincoln's War:
☞ ". . . what can I do more than I am doing? I would give my poor life gladly, if it would bring peace and good-will to the two countries; but it would not. It is with your own people you should labor [to stop the bloodshed]. It is they who desolate our homes, burn our wheat fields, break

the wheels of wagons carrying away our women and children, and destroy supplies meant for our sick and wounded. At your door lies all the misery and the crime of this war, and it is a fearful, fearful account."[232]

☛ "There was no humane course but to exchange prisoners according to the laws of war. With this the Government of the United States refused to comply, lest it might be construed into an acknowledgment of belligerent rights on our part, which would explode their theory of insurrectionary combinations, tend to restore more correct views of the rights and powers of the States, and expose in its true light their efforts to establish the supreme and unlimited sovereignty of the General Government. . . .Upon [this fraudulent theory's] . . . strict maintenance depended the success of their bloody revolution to secure absolute supremacy over the States."[233]

☛ "To supply medicines which were declared by the enemy to be contraband of war [and which were prevented from reaching us by Lincoln's illegal naval blockade], our medical department had to seek in the forest for substitutes, and to add surgical instruments and appliances to the small stock on hand as best they could."[234]

How the South adapted to warfare:
☛ ". . . the individuality, self-reliance, and habitual use of small arms by the people of the South was a substitute for military training . . ."[235]

☛ "Happy would it have been if the equal rights of the people of all the States to the enjoyment of territory acquired by the common treasure could have been recognized at the proper time! There would then have been no secession and no war."[236]

Toward the end of Lincoln's War, Davis—like Robert E. Lee, Patrick R. Cleburne, and thousands of other high-ranking Confederates—enthusiastically advocated officially enlisting blacks in the army (hundreds of thousands had been fighting unofficially since the start of the War). It was Lincoln's "theory" that blacks were not smart enough or brave enough to handle weapons and fight, which is one of the main reasons the U.S. president refused to allow blacks to enroll in the Union army until halfway through his War. When a few of Lincoln's racist supporters reprimanded Davis for advocating black enlistment, he shot back with the following reply:
☛ "If the Confederacy falls, there should be written on its tombstone, 'Died of a Theory.'"[237]

On Yankee war crimes:
☛ "Our people had been declared to be combinations of insurrectionists, and more than one hundred and fifty thousand men had been called to arms to invade our territory; our ports were [unconstitutionally] blockaded for the destruction of our regular commerce, and we had been threatened with denunciation as pirates if we molested a vessel of the United States, and some of our citizens had been confined in cells to await the punishment of piracy; one of our States [Virginia] was [unlawfully] rent asunder and a new State [West Virginia] constructed out of the fragment; every proposition for a peaceful solution of pending issues had been spurned."[238]

On Yankee war crimes:
☛ "An indiscriminate warfare had been waged upon our peaceful citizens, their dwellings burned and their crops destroyed; a law had been passed imposing a penalty of forfeiture on the owner of any faithful slave who gave military or naval service to the Confederacy, and forbidding military commanders to interfere for the restoration of fugitives; the United States Government had refused to agree to an exchange of prisoners, and suffered those we had captured to languish in captivity; it had falsely represented us in every court of Europe, to defeat our efforts to obtain a recognition from foreign powers; it had seized a portion of the members of the Legislature of one State and confined them in a distant military prison, because they were thought merely to sympathize with us, though they had not committed an overt act; it had refused all the propositions of another State for a peaceful neutrality, invaded her and seized important positions, where not even a disturbance of the peace had occurred, and perpetrated the most despotic outrages on her people; it rejected the most conciliatory terms offered for the sake of peace by the Governor of another State, claimed for itself an unrestricted right to move and station its troops whenever and wherever its officers might think it to be desirable, and persisted in its aggressions until the people were involved in conflicts, and a provisional government became necessary for their protection."[239]

On Yankee war crimes:
☛ "Within the Northern States, which professed to be struggling to maintain the Union, the Constitution, its only bond, and the laws made in pursuance of it, were in peaceful, undisputed existence; yet even there the [Lincoln] Government ruled with the tyrant's hand, and the provisions for the freedom of speech, freedom of the press, and the personal liberty of the

citizen, were daily violated, and these sacred rights of man suppressed by military force."[240]

On Yankee war crimes:

☞ "[Due to] sectional hate and the vain conceit of newly acquired power . . . [both Northern and Southern] citizens were arrested without due process of law, deported to distant States, and incarcerated without assigned cause. All this by persons acting under authority of the United States Government, but in disregard of the United States Constitution, which provides that 'no person shall be held to answer for a capital or otherwise infamous crime, unless on a presentment or an indictment of a grand jury, nor be deprived of life, liberty, or property without due process of law.' 'The right of the people to be secure in their persons, houses, papers, and effects, against unreasonable searches and seizures shall not be violated.' These provisions were of no avail to protect the citizens from the outrages, because those who derived their authority from the Constitution used that authority to violate its guarantees."[241]

On Yankee war crimes:

☞ "It has been stated that the rule upon which the United States Government was conducting affairs was entirely revolutionary. Its efforts to clothe the Government of the Union with absolute power involved the destruction of the rights of the States and the subversion of the Constitution. Hence on every occasion the provisions of the Constitution afforded no protection to the citizens: their rights were spurned; their persons were seized and imprisoned beyond the reach of friends; their houses sacked and burned. If they pleaded the Constitution, the Government of the Constitution was deaf to them, unsheathed its sword, and said the Union was at stake; and the Constitution, which was the compact of union, must stand aside. This was indeed a revolution. A constitutional government of limited powers derived from the people was transformed into a military despotism. The Northern people were docile as sheep under the change, reminding one of the words of the Psalmist: 'All we, like sheep, have gone astray.'"[242]

☞ "Who was to be the umpire in such a case? Not the United States Government, for it was the creature of the States; it possessed no inherent, original sovereignty. The Constitution says, 'The powers not delegated to the United States by the Constitution, nor prohibited by it to the States, are reserved to the States respectively, or to the people.' The umpireship is, therefore, expressly on the side of the States, or the people."[243]

On Lincoln and his followers' illegal and unconstitutional creation of the state of "West Virginia" in the western portion of Virginia:

☛ "Will any intelligent person assert that the consent of the State of Virginia was given to the formation of this new State, or that the government of [Lincoln supporter, Liberal, and governor of Virginia] Francis H. Pierpont held the true and lawful jurisdiction of the State of Virginia? Yet the Congress of the United States asserted in the act above quoted that 'the Legislature of Virginia did give its consent to the formation of a new State within the jurisdiction of the State of Virginia.' This was not true, but was an attempt, by an act of [the U.S.] Congress, to aid a fraud and perpetuate a monstrous usurpation. For there is no grant of power to Congress in the Constitution nor in the American theory of government to justify it. If it is said that the government of Francis H. Pierpont was the only one recognized by Congress as the government of the State of Virginia, that does not alter the fact. The recognition of Congress can not make a State of an organization which is not a State. There is no grant of power to Congress in the Constitution for that purpose. If it is said that the government of Francis H. Pierpont was established by the only qualified voters in the State of Virginia, that is as equally unfounded as the other assertions. Neither the Congress of the United States nor the Government of the United States can determine the qualifications of voters at an election for delegates to a State Constitutional Convention, or for the choice of State officers. There was no grant of power either to the President [Lincoln] or to Congress for that purpose. All these efforts were usurpations, by which it was sought, through groundless fabrications, to reach certain ends, and they add to the multitude of deeds which constitute the crime committed against States and the liberties of the people.

"When the question of the admission of West Virginia was before the House of Representatives of the United States Congress, [Yankee Liberal] Mr. Thaddeus Stevens, of Pennsylvania, declared, with expiatory frankness, that he would not stultify himself by claiming the act to be constitutional. He said, 'We know that it is not constitutional, but it is necessary.'"[244]

On Yankee war crimes and outrages in Tennessee:

☛ "On the capture of Nashville, on February 25, 1862, [Tennessee Unionist]

Andrew Johnson was made military Governor of Tennessee, with the rank of brigadier-general, and immediately entered on the duties of his office. This step was taken by the President of the United States under the pretense of executing that provision of the Constitution which is in these words: 'The United States shall guarantee to every State in this Union a republican form of government.'

"The administration was conducted according to the will and pleasure of the Governor, which was the supreme law. Public officers were required to take an oath of allegiance to the United States Government, and upon refusal were expelled from office. Newspaper-offices were closed, and their publication suppressed. Subsequently the offices were sold out under the provisions of the confiscation act. All persons using 'treasonable and seditious' language were arrested and required to take the oath of allegiance to the Government of the United States, and give bonds for the future, or to go into exile. Clergymen, upon their refusal to take the oath, were confined in the prisons until they could be sent away. School-teachers and editors and finally large numbers of private citizens were arrested and held until they took the oath. Conflicts became frequent in the adjacent country. Murders and the violent destruction of property ensued.

"On October 21,1862, an order for an election of members of the United States Congress in the ninth and tenth State districts was issued. Every voter was required to give satisfactory evidence of 'loyalty' to the Northern Government."[245]

On Yankee war crimes and outrages in Louisiana:
☛ "Peaceful and aged citizens, unresisting captives, and noncombatants, were confined at hard labor with chains attached to their limbs, and held in dungeons and fortresses; others were subjected to a like degrading punishment for selling medicine to the sick soldiers of the Confederacy. The soldiers of the invading force were incited and encouraged by general orders to insult and outrage the wives and mothers and sisters of the citizens; and helpless women were torn from their homes and subjected to solitary confinement, some in fortresses and prisons—and one, especially, on an island of barren sand, under a tropical sun—and were fed with loathsome rations and exposed to vile insults. Prisoners of war, who surrendered to the naval forces of the United States on the agreement that they should be released on parole, were seized and kept in close confinement. Repeated pretexts were sought or invented for plundering the inhabitants of the captured city, by fines levied and collected under threat

of imprisonment at hard labor with ball and chain. The entire population were forced to elect between starvation by the confiscation of all their property and taking an oath against their conscience to bear allegiance to the invader. Egress from the city was refused to those whose fortitude stood the test, and even to lone and aged women and to helpless children; and, after being ejected from their houses and robbed of their property, they were left to starve in the streets or subsist on charity. The slaves were driven from the plantations in the neighborhood of New Orleans, until their owners consented to share their crops with the commanding [Yankee] General, his brother, and other [Union] officers. When such consent had been extorted, the slaves were restored to the plantations and compelled to work under the bayonets of a guard of United States soldiers. Where that partnership was refused, armed expeditions were sent to the plantations to rob them of everything that could be removed; and even slaves too aged and infirm for work were, in spite of their entreaties, forced from the homes provided by their owners, and driven to wander helpless on the highway. By an order (No. 91), the entire property in that part of Louisiana west of the Mississippi River was sequestrated for confiscation, and officers were assigned to the duty, with orders to gather up and collect the personal property, and turn over to the proper officers, upon their receipts, such of it as might be required for the use of the United States army; and to bring the remainder to New Orleans, and cause it to be sold at public auction to the highest bidders. This was an order which, if it had been executed, would have condemned to punishment, by starvation, at least a quarter of a million of persons, of all ages, sexes, and conditions. The African slaves, also, were not only incited to insurrection by every license and encouragement, but numbers of them were armed for a servile war, which in its nature, as exemplified in other lands, far exceeds the horrors and merciless atrocities of savages. In many instances the [Yankee] officers were active and zealous agents in the commission of these crimes, and no instance was known of the refusal of any one of them to participate in the outrages."[246]

☞ "[Another example of the many Yankee atrocities committed in Louisiana] was the cold-blooded execution of William B. Mumford on June 7th [1862]. He was an unresisting and noncombatant captive, and there was no offense ever alleged to have been committed by him subsequent to the date of the capture of the city. He was charged with aiding and abetting certain persons in hauling down a United States flag hoisted on the [New Orleans] mint, which was left there by a boat's crew on the morning of

April 26ᵗʰ, and five days before the military occupation of the city. He was tried before a military commission, sentenced, and afterward hanged."[247]

On the war crimes of Union General John Pope:
☛ "[In July 1862] Major-General Pope, in command of the United States forces near Washington, issued a general order directing the murder of our peaceful inhabitants as spies, if found quietly tilling the farms in his rear, even outside of his lines; and one of his brigadier-generals seized upon innocent and peaceful inhabitants to be held as hostages, to the end that they might be murdered in cold blood if any of his soldiers were killed by some unknown persons, whom he designated as 'bushwhackers.' Under this state of facts, I issued a general order, recognizing General Pope and his commissioned officers to be in the position which they had chosen for themselves—that of robbers and murderers, and not that of public enemies, entitled, if captured, to be considered as prisoners of war. Some of the military authorities of the United States seemed to suppose that better success would attend a savage war, in which no quarter was to be given and no age or sex to be spared, than had hitherto been secured by such hostilities as were alone recognized to be lawful by civilized men. We renounced our right of retaliation on the innocent, and continued to treat the soldiers of General Pope's army as prisoners of war, confining our repressive measures to the punishment only of commissioned officers as were willing participants in such crimes. General Pope was soon afterward removed from command."[248]

On the numerous unconstitutional Yankee crimes, such as poll rigging, in Kentucky:
☛ "In the State of Kentucky, the first open and direct measures taken by the Government of the United States for the subjugation of the State government and people, thereby to effect the emancipation of the slaves, consisted in an interference with the voters at the State election in August, 1863. This interference was by means of a military force [that is, armed Yankee soldiers] stationed at the polls to sustain and enforce the action of some of the servants of the Government of the United States, the object being to overawe the judges of election, secure the administration of a rigid oath of allegiance, and thereby the rejection of as many antagonistic votes as possible. Indeed, it was intended that none but so-called 'Union' men should vote—that is, men who were willing to approve of every measure which the Government of the United States might adopt to carry on the war and revolutionize the State. At the same time, no man was allowed to be a

candidate or to receive any votes unless he was a well-known advocate of the Government of the United States."[249]

On unconstitutional Yankee crimes and outrages in New York:
☛ "To show how the laws were disregarded, and how despotically the personal liberty of the citizen was invaded, let this example bear witness: The Secretary of State at Washington, William H. Seward, a favored son of the State of New York, would 'ring a little bell,' which brought to him a messenger, to whom was given a secret order to arrest and confine in Fort Lafayette a person designated. This order was sent by telegraph to the United States Marshal of the district in which would be found the person who was to be arrested. The arrest being forcibly made by the marshal with armed attendants without even the form of a warrant, the prisoner without the knowledge of any charge against him was conveyed to Fort Hamilton and turned over to the commandant. An aid with a guard of soldiers then conveyed him in a boat to Fort Lafayette and delivered him to the keeper in charge, who gave a receipt for the prisoner. He was then divested of any weapons, money, valuables, or papers in his possession. His baggage was opened and searched. A soldier then took him in charge to the designated quarter, which was a portion of one of the casemates for guns, lighted only from the port-hole, and occupied by seven or eight other prisoners. All were subjected to prison fare. Some were citizens of New York, and the others of different States. This manner of imprisonment was subsequently put under the direction of the [U.S.] Secretary of War, and continued at intervals until the close of the war."[250]

On Yankee atrocities across the Northern states:
☛ "A large number of . . . [unwarranted and illegal] arrests were made [by Lincoln] in Ohio, newspapers were suspended, and editors imprisoned. Like scenes were very numerous in Indiana and Illinois. In Pennsylvania arrests were made, newspapers suspended, editors imprisoned, and offices destroyed. In New Hampshire, Vermont, and Wisconsin many similar scenes occurred. The [U.S.] provost-marshal system was used as a weapon of vindictiveness against influential citizens of opposite political views throughout all the Northern States. No one of such persons knew when he was safe. A complaint of his neighbors, supported by affidavit of 'disloyal' words spoken or 'disloyal' acts approved, received prompt attention from all [U.S.] marshals. Everything was brought into subjection to the will of the Government of the United States and its military officers."[251]

LOCHLAINN SEABROOK 〜 95

☛ "In view of all the facts here presented relative to the Northern States, let the reader answer where the sovereignty *de facto* resided. Most clearly in the Government of the United States. That presided over the ballot-box, held the keys of the prisons, arrested all citizens at its pleasure, suspended or suppressed newspapers, and did whatever it pleased under the declaration that the public welfare required it. But, under the principles of American liberty, the sovereignty is inherent in the people as an unalienable right; and, for the preservation and protection of this and other rights, the State governments were instituted. If, therefore, the people have lost this inherent sovereignty, it is evident that the State governments have failed to afford that protection for which they were instituted. If they have thus failed, it has been in consequence of their subversion and loss of power to fulfill the object for which they were established. This subversion was achieved when the [U.S.] General Government, under the [Lincolnian] pretext of preserving the Union, made war on its creators the States, thus changing the nature of the Federal Union, which could rightfully be done only by the sovereign, the people of the States, in like manner as it was originally formed. If they should permit their sovereignty to be usurped and themselves to be subjugated, individuals might remain, States could not. Of their wreck a nation might be built, but there could not be a Union, for that implies entities united, and of a State which has lost its sovereignty there may only be written, 'It was.'"[252]

On how Confederate soldiers must approach the enemy:
☛ "To show ourselves worthy of the inheritance bequeathed to us by the patriots of the [American] Revolution, we must emulate that heroic devotion which made reverse to them but the crucible in which their patriotism was refined."[253]

In a letter addressed to U.S. President Abraham Lincoln:
☛ ". . . I have to complain of the conduct of your officers and troops in many parts of the country, who violate all the rules of war, by carrying on hostilities, not only against armed foes, but against non-combatants, aged men, women, and children; while others not only seize such property as is required for the use of your forces, but destroy all private property within their reach, even agricultural implements; and openly avow the purpose of seeking to subdue the population of the districts where they are operating, by the starvation that must result from the destruction of standing crops and agricultural tools.

"Still, again, others of your officers in different districts have recently taken the lives of prisoners who fell into their power, and justify their act by asserting a right to treat as spies the military officers and enlisted men under my command, who may penetrate for hostile purposes into States claimed by me to be engaged in the warfare now waged against the United States, and claimed by the latter as having refused to engage in such warfare.

"I have heretofore, on different occasions, been forced to make complaint of these outrages, and to ask from you that you should either avow or disclaim having authorized them, and have failed to obtain such answer as the usages of civilized warfare require to be given in such cases.

"These usages justify, and indeed require, redress by retaliation, as the proper means of repressing such cruelties as are not permitted in warfare between Christian peoples."[254]

☛ ". . . the Government of the United States, in order to effect our subjugation, devastated our fields, destroyed our crops, broke up our railroads, and thus interrupted our means of transportation, and reduced our people, our armies, and consequently their soldiers, who were our prisoners, all alike, to the most straitened condition for food. Our medicines for the sick were exhausted, and, contrary to the usage of civilized nations, they were made, by our enemy, contraband of war. After causing these and other distressing events—of which Atlanta, where the women and children were driven into the fields and their houses burned, and Columbia, with its smoking and plundered ruins, were prominent examples—after every effort to excite our slaves to servile war—this Government of the United States turned to the Northern people, and, charging us with atrocious cruelties to their sons, who were our prisoners, appealed to them again and again to recruit the armies and take vengeance upon us by our abject subjugation or entire extermination. It was the last effort of the usurper to save himself."[255]

☛ "Whatever of hope some may have entertained that a returning sense of justice would remove the danger with which our rights were threatened, and render it possible to preserve the Union of the constitution, must have been dispelled by the malignity and barbarity of the Northern States in the prosecution of the existing war. The confidence of the most hopeful among us must have been destroyed by the disregard they have recently exhibited for all the time honored bulwarks of civil and religious liberty. [Northern bastiles] filled with prisoners, arrested without civil process or indictment duly found; the writ of *habeas corpus* suspended by [Lincoln's] Executive mandate; a State Legislature controlled by the imprisonment of members whose avowed principles suggested to the Federal Executive that there might be another added to the list of seceded States; elections held under threats of a military power; civil officers, peaceful citizens and gentle women incarcerated for opinion's sake, proclaimed the incapacity of our late associates [to the North] to administer a government as free, liberal and humane as that established for our common use."[256]

☛ ". . . to the bold allegations of ill-treatment of prisoners on our side, and humane treatment and adequate supplies on that of our opponents, it is only necessary to offer two facts: First, the report of the [U.S.] Secretary of War, Edward M. Stanton, made on July 19, 1866, shows that, of all the prisoners in our hands during the war, only 22,576 died; while, of the prisoners in our opponents' hands, 26,246 died. Second, the official report of Surgeon-General Barnes, an officer of the United States Government, states that, in round numbers, the number of Confederate States prisoners in their hands amounted to 220,000, the number of United States prisoners in our hands amounted to 270,000. Thus, out of the 270,000 in our hands, 22,000 died; while of the 220,000 of our soldiers in their hands, 26,000 died. Thus, more than twelve per cent of the prisoners in our opponents' hands died, and less than nine per cent of the prisoners in our hands died."[257]

☛ "[When the Confederate Government] pleaded for peace, the United States Government deceptively delayed to answer, while making ready for war. To the calm judgment of mankind is submitted the question, Who was responsible for the war between the States?"[258]

☛ "I predicted war, not because our right to secede and to form a government of our own was not indisputable and clearly defined in the . . . declaration which rests the right to govern on the consent of the governed, but saw that the wickedness of the North would precipitate a war upon us."[259]

14

THE SOUTHERN PEOPLE

☛ "The people of the seceded States had loved the Union. Shoulder to shoulder with the people of the other States, they had bled for its liberties and its honor."[260]

☛ "[At the start of Lincoln's War a] marked characteristic of the Southern people was individuality, and time was needful to teach them that the terrible machine, a disciplined army, must be made of men who had surrendered their freedom of will."[261]

☛ "[Concerning] those [Confederate] regiments which have for so long a time been serving in the field. They have stood before the foe on many hard-fought fields, and have proven their courage and devotion on all. They have won the admiration of the army and of the country. And here I to-day repeat a compliment I have heard which, although it seems to partake of levity, appears an illustration of the esteem in which [we] Mississippians are held. It happened that several persons were conversing of a certain battle, and one of them remarked that the Mississippians did not run. "Oh! No!" said another, "Mississippians never run."[262]

Another view of Davis' library at "Beauvoir."

☛ "You have now in the field old men and gentle boys who have braved all the terrors and the dangers of war. I remember an instance of one of these, a brave and gallant youth, who, I was told, was but sixteen years of age. In one of those bloody battles by which the soil of Virginia has been consecrated to liberty, he was twice wounded, and each time bound up the wound with his own hands, while refusing to leave the field. A third time he was struck, and the lifeblood flowed in a crimson stream from his breast. His brother came to him to minister to his wants, but the noble boy said: 'Brother, you cannot do me any good now; go where you can do the Federals most harm.' Even then, while lying on the ground, his young life fast ebbing away, he cocked his rifle, and aimed it to take one last shot at the enemy. And so he died, a hero and a martyr."[263]

☞ "The heart of even a noble enemy must be moved at the spectacle of [our Confederate] citizens defending their homes, with muskets of obsolete patterns and shot-guns, against an invader having all the modern improvements in arms."[264]

To his fellow Southerners just days before Lee's surrender:
☞ "It is . . . unwise and unworthy of us, as patriots engaged in a most sacred cause to allow out energies to falter, our spirits to grow faint, or our efforts to become relaxed under reverses however calamitous."[265]

☞ "The theory that [our Southern people] . . . owed allegiance to their respective States was founded on the fact that the Federal Government was of the States . . ."[266]

☞ "If . . . we should ever be compelled to a temporary withdrawal from [Virginia] . . . or those of any other border State, again and again will we return, until the baffled and exhausted enemy shall abandon in despair his endless and impossible task of making slaves of a people resolved to be free."[267]

☞ ". . . the people of the Confederacy plainly saw that the ideas and interests of the [Lincoln] Administration were to gain by war the empire that would enable it to trample on the Constitution which it professed to defend and maintain."[268]

☞ ". . . we [Southerners] are brethren, not in name, merely, but in fact—men of one flesh, one bone, one interest, one purpose . . ."[269]

15

YANKEES

☞ "How can a people who glory in a Declaration of Independence which broke the slumbers of a world declare that men united in defense of liberty, property, and the pursuit of happiness are 'traitors'?"[270]

☞ "It has been my fortune to witness it [Lincoln's War] in all its terrors; in a part of the country where old men have been torn from their homes, carried into captivity, and immured in distant dungeons, and where delicate women have been insulted by a brutal soldiery, and forced even to cook for the dirty Federal invaders; where property has been wantonly destroyed, the country ravaged, and every outrage committed. And it is with these people that our fathers formed a union and a solemn contract. There is indeed a difference between the two peoples. Let no man hug the delusion that there can be renewed association between them. Our enemies are a traditionless and homeless race; from the time of [Oliver] Cromwell to the present moment they have been disturbers of the peace of the world."[271]

Davis in his favorite seat, on the waterfront at "Beauvoir."

☞ "They waged an indiscriminate war upon all: private houses in isolated retreats were bombarded and burned; grain-crops in the field were consumed by the torch; and, when the torch was not applied, careful labor was bestowed to render complete the destruction of every article of use or ornament remaining in private dwellings after their female inhabitants had fled from the insults of brutal soldiers; a petty war was made on the sick, including women and children, by carefully devised measures to prevent them from obtaining the necessary medicines. Were these the appropriate means by which to execute the laws, and in suppressing rioters to secure tranquillity and preserve a voluntary union? Was this a government resting on the consent of the governed?"[272]

To his fellow Southerners:
☞ "You have been involved in a war waged [by the Yanks] for the gratification of the lust of power and aggrandizement, for your conquest and your subjugation, with a malignant ferocity, and with a disregard and a contempt of the usages of civilisation, entirely unequalled in history. Such, I have ever warned you, were the characteristics of the Northern people—of those with whom our ancestors entered into a Union of consent, and with whom they formed a constitutional compact. And yet, such was the attachment of our people for that Union, such their devotion to it, that those who desired preparation to be made for the inevitable conflict, were denounced as men who wished to destroy the Union. After what has happened during the last two years, my only wonder is, that we consented to live for so long a time in association with such miscreants, and have loved so much a Government rotten to the core. Were it ever to be proposed again to enter into a Union with such a people, I could no more consent to do it than to trust myself in a den of thieves."[273]

On the character of Yankee soldiers:
☞ "They have bombarded undefended [Southern] villages without giving notice to women and children to enable them to escape, and in one instance selected the night as the period when they might surprise them most effectually whilst asleep and unsuspicious of danger."[274]

☞ "An amazing insensibility seemed to possess a portion of the Northern people as to the crisis before them. They would not realize that their purpose of supremacy would be so resolutely resisted; that, if persisted in, it must be carried to the extent of bloodshed in sectional war. With them the lust of dominion was stronger than the sense of justice or of the fraternity and the equal rights of the States, which the Union was formed to secure, and so they were blind to palpable results."[275]

16

AFTER LINCOLN'S WAR

On his May 1865 plans to continue the War "indefinitely" after Lee surrendered:

☛ "When I left [the city of] Washington, Georgia, with the small party . . . my object was to go to the south far enough to pass below the points reported to be occupied by Federal troops, and then turn to the west, cross the Chattahoochie [River], and then go on to meet the forces still supposed to be in the field in Alabama. If, as now seemed probable, there should be no prospect of a successful resistance east of the Mississippi, I intended then to cross to the trans-Mississippi Department, where I believed Generals Edmund Kirby Smith and John Bankhead Magruder [as well as Generals Dabney Herndon Maury, Nathan Bedford Forrest, and Richard Taylor] would continue to uphold our cause. . . . To this hope I persistently clung, and, if our independence could not be achieved, so much, at least, I trusted might be gained."[276]

Richmond, Virginia, in April 1865, the month Lincoln finally managed to violently and illegally coerce the South into rejoining what the Founding Fathers intended to be a "voluntary Union of friendly states."

On his illegal arrest and unconstitutional imprisonment after the War:

☛ "Bitter tears have been shed by the gentle, and stern reproaches have been made by the magnanimous, on account of the needless torture to which I was subjected, and the heavy fetters riveted upon me, while in a stone casemate and surrounded by a strong guard; but all these were less excruciating than the mental agony my captors were able to inflict. It was long before I was permitted to hear from my wife and children, and this, and things like this, was the power which education added to savage cruelty . . .”277

☛ “When the Confederate soldiers laid down their arms and went home, all hostilities against the power of the Government of the United States ceased. The powers delegated in the compact of 1787 by these States, i.e., by the people thereof, to a central organization to promote their general welfare, had been used for their devastation and subjugation. It was conceded, as the result of the contest, that the United States Government was stronger in resources than the Confederate Government, and that the Confederate States had not achieved their independence.

“Nothing remained to be done but for the sovereigns, the people of each State, to assert their authority and restore order. If the principle of the sovereignty of the people, the cornerstone of all our institutions, had survived and was still in force, it was necessary only that the people of each State should reconsider their ordinances of secession, and again recognize the Constitution of the United States as the supreme law of the land. This simple process would have placed the Union on its original basis, and have restored that which had ceased to exist, the Union by consent. Unfortunately, such was not the intention of the conqueror. The Union of free-wills and brotherly hearts, under a compact ordained by the people, was not his object. Henceforth there was to be established a Union of force. Sovereignty was to pass from the people to the Government of the United States, and to be upheld by those who had furnished the money and the soldiers for the war.”278

☛ “Having thus stripped each Confederate State of all civil government, it was asserted that the Constitution declares that the United States shall guarantee to each State a republican form of government. But to guarantee is not to create, to organize, or to bring into existence. This can be done for a State government only by the free and unconstrained action of the whole people of a State. The creation of such a government is beyond the powers of the Government of the United States. . . . After a republican government has been instituted by the people, the Constitution requires the United States to guarantee its existence, and thereby forbids them or their Government to overthrow it and set up a creature of its own. The duty to guarantee commands the preservation of that which already exists. Such were the governments of the Confederate States before the war and after the war. Thus the power granted in the Constitution to preserve and guarantee State governments was perverted [by Lincoln] to overthrow and destroy republican governments, and to erect in their places military Governors, Legislatures, and judicial tribunals."[279]

☛ "When the war ceased, the pretext on which it had been waged could no longer be alleged."[280]

☛ "[I have repeatedly proven] by historical authority that each of the States, as sovereign parties to the compact of Union, had the reserved power to secede from it whenever it was found not to answer the ends for which it was established. If this has been done, it follows that the war, on the part of the Government of the United States, was a war of aggression and usurpation; and on the part of the South was for the defence of an inherent and unalienable right."[281]

☛ "With the cessation of all hostilities against the power of the Government of the United States nothing remained to be done but for the sovereigns, the people of each State, to assert their authority and to restore order. If the principle of the sovereignty of the people—the corner-stone of our political institutions—had survived and was still in force, it was necessary only that the people of each State should reconsider and revoke their ordinances of secession, and again recognize the Constitution of the United States as the supreme law of the land. This simple process would have placed the Union on its original basis, and have restored what had ceased to exist—the Union by consent. Unfortunately, such was not the intention of the conqueror [Lincoln]. The union of free wills and brotherly hearts, under a compact ordained by the people, was not his object. Henceforth there was to be established a Union by force. Sovereignty was to pass from the people to the Government of the United States, and to be upheld by those who had furnished the money and the soldiers for the war."[282]

☛ "In asserting the right of secession, it has not been my wish to incite to its exercise. I recognize the fact that the war showed it to be impracticable; but this did not prove it to be wrong; and now that it may not be again attempted, and that the Union may promote the general welfare, it is needful that the truth, the whole truth, should be known, so that crimination and recrimination may forever cease; and then, on the basis of fraternity and faithful regard for the rights of the States, there may be written on the arch of the Union, *Esto perpetua* ['It is perpetual'].["283]

☛ "The principle for which we contended is bound to reassert itself, though it may be at another time and in another form."[284]

☛ "Let us, the survivors . . . not fail to do credit to the generous credulity which could not understand how, in violation of the compact of Union, a war could be waged against the States, or why they should be invaded because their people had deemed it necessary to withdraw from an association which had failed to fulfill the ends for which they had entered into it, and which, having been broken to their injury by the other parties, had ceased to be binding upon them. It is a satisfaction to know that the calamities which have befallen the Southern States were the result of their credulous reliance on the power of the Constitution, that, if it failed to protect their rights, it would at least suffice to prevent an attempt at coercion, if, in the last resort, they peacefully withdrew from the Union."[285]

On whether Lincoln's War served any purpose:
☛ "Let the recital of the invasion of the reserved powers of the States, or the people, and the perversion of the republican form of government guaranteed to each State by the Constitution, answer the question. For the deplorable fact of the war, for the cruel manner in which it was waged, for the sad physical and yet sadder moral results it produced, the reader of these pages, I hope, will admit that the South, in the forum of conscience, stands fully acquitted."[286]

☛ "The war was one in which fundamental principles were involved; and, as force decides no truth, hence the issue is still undetermined . . . . We have laid aside our swords; we have ceased our hostility; we have conceded the physical strength of the Northern States. But the question still lives, and all nations and peoples that adopt a confederated agent of government will become champions of our cause. While contemplating the Northern States—with their Federal Constitution gone, ruthlessly destroyed—under the tyrant's plea of 'necessity,' their State sovereignty made a byword, and their people absorbed in an aggregated mass, no longer, as their fathers left them, protected by reserved rights against usurpation—the question naturally arises: On which side was the victory? Let the verdict of mankind decide."[287]

☞ "Although the Confederate armies may have left the field, although the citizen soldiers may have retired to the pursuits of peaceful life, although the Confederate States may have renounced their new Union, they have proved their indestructibility by resuming their former places in the old one, where, by the organic law, they could only be admitted as republican, equal, and sovereign States of the Union. And, although the Confederacy as an organization may have ceased to exist as unquestionably as though it had never been formed, the fundamental principles, the eternal truths, uttered when our colonies in 1776 declared their independence, on which the Confederation of 1781 and the Union of 1788 were formed, and which animated and guided in the organization of the Confederacy of 1861, yet live, and will survive, however crushed they may be by despotic force, however deep they may be buried under the debris of crumbling States, however they may be disavowed by the time-serving and the fainthearted; yet I believe they have the eternity of truth, and that in God's appointed time and place they will prevail."[288]

☞ "The contest is not over, the strife is not ended. It has only entered on a new and enlarged arena. The champions of constitutional liberty must spring to the struggle, like the armed men from the seminated dragon's teeth, until the Government of the United States is brought back to its constitutional limits, and the tyrant's plea of 'necessity' is bound in chains strong as adamant."[289]

☞ "Tis been said that I should apply to the United States for a pardon, but repentance must precede the right of pardon, and I have not repented. . . . I deliberately say, if it were to do over again, I would again do just as I did in 1861."[290]

17

RECONSTRUCTION

☛ "Illegal, unjust, and vindictive as were . . . [the] gross usurpations of the Congress of the United States in their immediate results [during Lincoln's War on the South], the consequences which followed were still more disastrous. When [under Reconstruction] the late Confederate States were restored to representation in Congress [that is, reunionized], a large portion of their white citizens remained disfranchised, and the political power of each was in the hands of the blacks and the remnant of the whites. Nor was the [Northern] military force withdrawn, but it was placed in convenient localities, under the pretext of maintaining order, but in reality to sustain the new rulers. It must be manifest that the sovereignty of the people was now extinct, and those ruled who had the bayonets on their side. With the disfranchised were the intelligence, the virtue, and the political experience; with the voters were the ignorance, the lawless passions, and soon a body of political adventurers from the Northern States, greedy for power and plunder. These quickly won for themselves the distinctive epithet of 'carpet-baggers.' The governments under the control of such popular sovereigns demonstrated the vindictiveness rather than wisdom of Congress, and soon brought forth their natural fruits of anarchy, fraud, and crime."[291]

The title of this 1875 anti-Reconstruction cartoon, from a New York newspaper, is "Grant's Last Outrage in Louisiana." So-called "Reconstruction" lasted from 1865 to 1877, most of it under the anti-South U.S. President Ulysses S. Grant, seen here bottom right.

On life in the South under so-called "Reconstruction":

☛ "[Yankee military] commissioners were appointed over sub-districts [of all the former Confederate states] for the suppression of disorder and violence, for the protection of all persons in their so-called rights of person and property, and clothed with all the powers of justices of a county or police magistrates of a city. The State was also divided into sub-districts, and commanders appointed over the same. These [Yankee] officers were empowered to exercise a general supervision over the military commissioners, and to furnish them, when necessary, with sufficient military force to enable them to discharge their duties. Further orders relative to the qualification of voters were issued by the major-general, in which it was declared that 'all persons who voluntarily joined the rebel army, and all persons in that army, whether volunteers or conscripts, who committed voluntarily any hostile act, were thereby engaged in insurrection or rebellion; and all who voted for the ordinance of secession, gave aid and comfort to the enemy. Also all who voluntarily furnished supplies of food, or clothing, arms, ammunition, horses, or mules, or any other material of war, participated in the rebellion,' and were disfranchised."[292]

Examples of the Yankee dictatorship that was unconstitutionally imposed on the South during Reconstruction:

☛ "A lecture on the 'Chivalry of the South,' advertised to be delivered in Lynchburg, was suppressed by the order of the [Yankee] post commander at that place. A warning was given by the [Yankee] major-general to the editor of the Richmond *Times*, which said, 'The efforts of your paper to foster enmity, create disorder, and lead to violence, can no longer be tolerated.'. . . All armed organizations in the State were disbanded. [And yet] inflammatory meetings of freedmen and those who sought their political alliance were [allowed to be] held in different parts of the State."[293]

☛ "Where now were the unalienable rights of man, and the sovereignty of the people, with their safeguards; a Constitution with limited powers, the reserved rights of the States, and the supremacy of law equally over both rulers and ruled? All were gone."[294]

☛ "It will be seen that, through all these proceedings, the Government of the United States controlled as the sovereign, and the sovereignty of the people was extinct. . . .The uppermost then had come to be the undermost now, and that which was nothing then had grown to be over all now. Will it always be thus? Was the inherent sovereignty of the people destroyed by shot and shell?"[295]

☛ "The intelligent reader must perceive that this invasion of the natural and unalienable rights of man, the subjugation of the sovereignty of the people, the monstrous usurpations of powers not granted in the Constitution, the trampling under foot of the reserved rights of the States, the disregard of the supremacy of law, and the assumption of the sovereignty of the Government of the United States as the corner-stone of our future political edifice, is a revolution in our system of Government, deep-seated, reaching to the foundations, and sending the poisonous waters of despotism throughout all the branches fed from this fountain. The Confederate States resisted it from the beginning. They drew their swords for the sovereignty of the people, and they fought for the maintenance of their State governments in all their reserved rights and powers, as the only true and natural guardians of the unalienable rights of their citizens, among which the most sacred is, that only the consent of the governed can give vitality and existence to any civil or political institution."[296]

☛ "The day has come in which mankind behold this Government founding its highest claims to greatness and glory upon deeds done in utter violation of those rights which belonged to its own citizens in every State, North and South. The palladium of the freeman, the Bills of Rights, the limitations of power, the written Constitutions, have all lost their sacred authority, and not a man or a State dare, single-handed, gainsay the will of the agency which, feeling power, has forgotten right. [The Lincoln government] . . . has put its hand on the ballot-box, and the declaration is made that it is not safe to trust the people to vote, except under the inspection of its authority, after the example set by the Roman emperors. When the cause was lost, what cause was it?   Not that of the South only, but the cause of constitutional government, of the supremacy of law, of the natural rights of man."[297]

18

QUOTES ABOUT

JEFFERSON DAVIS

☞ "Mr. Davis was a great President. In administering the affairs of the Confederate Government he displayed remarkable constructive and executive genius. Considering the resources at his command, all the Southern ports blockaded and without the recognition of any foreign nation,

Portrait of an American president: Jefferson Davis, to many citizens still our greatest chief executive.

with no opportunity to sell cotton abroad and import supplies in return, having to rely entirely upon the fields and strong arms of the home land, and constantly menaced by one of the greatest armies of the world, it was remarkable that the young nation could have survived a few months, instead of four memorable years. And much of that wonderful history is due to its Chief Executive."[298] *Bishop Charles B. Galloway*

☞ "If my opinion is worth anything, you can always say that few people could have done better than Mr. Davis. I know of none that could have done as well."[299] *Gen. Robert E. Lee, C.S.A.*

☞ "I could detain you all night correcting false impressions which have been industriously made against this great and good man. I know Jefferson Davis as I know few men. I have been near him in his public duties; I have seen him by his private fireside; I have witnessed his humble Christian devotions; and I challenge the judgment of history when I say, no people were ever led through the fiery struggle for liberty by a nobler, truer patriot; while the carnage of war and the trials of public life never revealed a purer and more beautiful Christian character."[300] *Georgia Senator Benjamin Harvey Hill*

☞ "Davis . . . impressed me that winter more agreeably than any Southern man I met. . . . he was a distinctly attractive as well as interesting personality. Of medium height and spare of figure, he had an essentially Southern face, but he was very much of a gentleman in his address—courteous, unpretending and yet quietly dignified. A man in no way aggressive, yet not to be trifled with. I instinctively liked him; and regret extremely that it was not my good fortune, then or later, to see more of him."[301] *Col. Charles Francis Adams, Jr., U.S.A. (great-grandson of U.S. President John Adams)*

☞ "I loved him as I have never loved any other man."[302] *Texas Senator John Henninger Reagan*

☞ "As the old body-servant of the late Jefferson Davis, my great desire was to be the driver of the remains of my old master to their last resting-place. Returning too late to join the white delegation from this city, I am deprived of the opportunity of showing my lasting appreciation for my best friend."[303] *James H. Jones*

☞ "We, the old servants and tenants of our beloved master, Hon. Jefferson Davis, have cause to mingle our tears over his death, who was always so kind and thoughtful of our peace and happiness. We extend to you our humble sympathy. Respectfully your old tenants and servants."[304] *Ned Gator, Tom McKinney, Grant McKinney, Mary Pendleton, Mary Archer, Elijah Martin, Wm. Nervis, Isabel Kitchens, Teddy Everson, Hy Garland, Laura Nick, Wm. Green, Gus Williams (and others)*

☞ "I think history will record him as one of the greatest men of the time. Every lost cause, you know, must have a scapegoat, and Mr. Davis has been chosen as such; he must take all the blame without any of the credit. I do not know any man in the Confederate States that could have conducted the war with the same success that he did."[305] *Gen. John Singleton Mosby, C.S.A.*

☛ "Those who knew Jefferson Davis in intimate relations honored him most and loved him. Genial and gentle, approachable to all, especially regardful of the humble and the lowly, affable in conversation, and enriching it from the amplest stores of a refined and cultured mind, he fascinated those who came within the circle of his society and endeared them to him. Reserved as to himself, he bore the afflictions of a diseased body with scant allusion even when it became needful to plead them in self-defense. With bandaged eyes and weak from suffering he would come from a couch of pain to vote on public issues, and for over twenty years, with the sight of one eye gone, he dedicated his labors to the vindication of the South from the aspersions which misconceptions and passions had engendered.

"At over four-score years he died, with his harness on, his pen yet bright and trenchant, his mental eye undimmed, his soul athirst for peace, truth, justice, and fraternity, breathing his last breath in clearing the memories of the Lost Confederacy!"[306] *Virginia Senator John Warwick Daniel*

☛ "Jefferson Davis deserves our reverence because he has stood for a quarter of a century in our place. He endured a cruel captivity for two years, and for the residue of that time has been the vicarious victim of obloquy and reproach due to us all, and heaped upon him alone by the press and people of the North. His fortitude and devotion to truth never failed. He endured not in silence, but with a protest which history has recorded, and will preserve as an emphatic vindication of the Confederacy which had perished, from malign aspersions on the motives of its friends, on the origin and causes of its formation, and on the purposes of justice and liberty, which inspired those who died in its defence, or who survived to illustrate its principles in doing the duties public and private which God in his providence assigned them to perform."[307] *Virginia Congressman John Randolph Tucker*

☛ "He was a man among men. He was not the cruel and hard-hearted man his enemies paint him. He was as brave as a lion, yet as gentle, as kind-hearted and tender as a woman."[308] *Alabama Governor Thomas Hill Watts*

☛ "Jefferson Davis will be mourned in millions of hearts this day. [The U.S.] Government will not render to him the pomp and circumstance of a great death; but his people will . . . He is our dead!"[309] *Southern journalist and orator Henry Woodfin Grady*

President Davis and his cabinet in 1861. From left to right: Stephen Russell Mallory (secretary of the Navy), Judah Philip Benjamin (attorney general), LeRoy Pope Walker (secretary of war), Jefferson Davis (president), Robert Edward Lee (general-in-chief of Confederate forces), John Henninger Reagan (postmaster general), Christopher Gustavus Memminger (secretary of the Treasury), Alexander Hamilton Stephens (vice president), Robert Augustus Toombs (secretary of state).

APPENDIX

Conservative Davis was one of America's most ardent and strict Constitutionalists. He would be appalled to see, for example, the modern Liberals' war on the First and Second Amendments. Below are Davis' core views on the Constitution, the states, and the central government. "I hold," he declared in 1881,

"1. That the States of which the American Union was formed, from the moment when they emerged from their colonial or provincial condition, became severally sovereign, free, and independent States—not one State, or nation.

"2. That the union formed under the Articles of Confederation was a compact between the States, in which these attributes of 'sovereignty, freedom, and independence,' were expressly asserted and guaranteed.

"3. That, in forming the 'more perfect union' of the Constitution, afterward adopted, the same contracting powers formed an amended compact, without any surrender of these attributes of sovereignty, freedom, and independence, either expressed or implied: on the contrary, that, by the tenth amendment to the Constitution, limiting the power of the Government to its express grants, they distinctly guarded against the presumption of a surrender of anything by implication.

"4. That political sovereignty resides, neither in individual citizens, nor in unorganized masses, nor in fractional subdivisions of a community, but in the people of an organized political body.

"5. That no 'republican form of government,' in the sense in which that expression is used in the Constitution, and was generally understood by the founders of the Union—whether it be the government of a State or of a confederation of States— is possessed of any sovereignty whatever, but merely exercises certain powers delegated by the sovereign authority of the people, and subject to recall and reassumption by the same authority that conferred them.

"6. That the 'people' who organized the first confederation, the people who dissolved it, the people who ordained and established the Constitution which succeeded it, the only people, in fine, known or referred to in the phraseology of that period—whether the term was used collectively or distributively—were the people of the respective States, each acting separately and with absolute independence of the others.

"7. That, in forming and adopting the Constitution, the States, or the people of the States—terms which, when used with reference to acts performed in a sovereign capacity, are precisely equivalent to each other—formed a new Government, but no new people; and that, consequently, no new sovereignty was created—for sovereignty in an American republic can belong only to a people, never to a government—and that the Federal Government is entitled to exercise only the powers delegated to it by the people of the respective States.

"8 That the term 'people,' in the preamble to the Constitution and in the tenth amendment, is used distributively; that the only 'people of the United States' known to the Constitution are the people of each State in the Union; that no such political community or corporate unit as one people of the United States then existed, has ever been organized, or yet exists; and that no political action by the people of the United States in the aggregate has ever taken place, or ever can take place, under the Constitution."[310]

NOTES

1. See Jones, TDMV, pp. 144, 200-201, 273.
2. See Seabrook, TAHSR, passim. See also, Pollard, LC, p. 178; Franklin, pp. 101, 111, 130, 149; Nicolay and Hay, ALCW, Vol. 1, p. 627.
3. For more on this topic, see Seabrook, ALWAL, JDWAC, passim.
4. See e.g., Seabrook, TQJD, pp. 30, 38, 76.
5. Seabrook, EYWTATCWIW, p. 13.
6. J. Davis, RFCG, Vol. 1, p. 229.
7. Seabrook, LRAL, pp. 918-938.
8. J. Davis, RFCG, Vol. 1, p. 97.
9. J. Davis, RFCG, Vol. 1, p. 143.
10. J. Davis, RFCG, Vol. 1, p. 63.
11. J. Davis, RFCG, Vol. 1, p. 141.
12. J. Davis, RFCG, Vol. 1, pp. 143-144.
13. J. Davis, RFCG, Vol. 1, pp. 152.
14. J. Davis, RFCG, Vol. 1, p. 146.
15. J. Davis, RFCG, Vol. 1, p. 232.
16. J. Davis, RFCG, Vol. 1, p. 325.
17. J. Davis, RFCG, Vol. 1, pp. 146-147.
18. J. Davis, RFCG, Vol. 1, p. 147.
19. J. Davis, RFCG, Vol. 1, p. 147.
20. J. Davis, RFCG, Vol. 1, p. 147.
21. J. Davis, RFCG, Vol. 1, p. 148.
22. J. Davis, RFCG, Vol. 1, pp. 325-326.
23. J. Davis, RFCG, Vol. 1, p. 65.
24. J. Davis, RFCG, Vol. 1, pp. 141-142.
25. J. Davis, RFCG, Vol. 1, p. 142.
26. J. Davis, RFCG, Vol. 1, p. 164.
27. J. Davis, RFCG, Vol. 1, p. 62.
28. J. Davis, RFCG, Vol. 1, p. 142.
29. J. Davis, RFCG, Vol. 1, pp. 142-143.
30. Victor, HCPMSR, Vol. 3, p. 39.
31. J. Davis, RFCG, Vol. 1, p. 156.
32. J. Davis, RFCG, Vol. 1, p. 606.
33. Victor, HCPMSR, Vol. 3, p. 38.
34. J. Davis, RFCG, Vol. 1, p. 545.
35. J. Davis, RFCG, Vol. 1, p. 127.
36. J. Davis, RFCG, Vol. 2, p. 368.
37. J. Davis, RFCG, Vol. 1, p. 322.
38. J. Davis, RFCG, Vol. 2, p. 175.
39. J. Davis, RFCG, Vol. 2, p. 451.
40. J. Davis, RFCG, Vol. 1, p. 322.
41. J. Davis, RFCG, Vol. 1, p. 220.
42. J. Davis, RFCG, Vol. 1, p. 67.
43. J. Davis, SHCSA, p. 48.
44. J. Davis, SHCSA, pp. 48-49.
45. J. Davis, SHCSA, p. 49.
46. J. Davis, SHCSA, p. 49.
47. J. Davis, RFCG, Vol. 1, pp. 21-22.
48. J. Davis, RFCG, Vol. 2, p. 451.
49. J. Davis, RFCG, Vol. 1, p. 183.
50. J. Davis, RFCG, Vol. 1, p. 195.
51. J. Davis, RFCG, Vol. 1, p. 209.
52. J. Davis, RFCG, Vol. 1, p. 2.

53. J. Davis, RFCG, Vol. 2, p. 452.
54. J. Davis, RFCG, Vol. 1, p. 216.
55. J. Davis, RFCG, Vol. 1, p. 530.
56. J. Davis, RFCG, Vol. 1, p. 590.
57. J. Davis, RFCG, Vol. 1, p. 614.
58. J. Davis, RFCG, Vol. 1, p. 618.
59. J. Davis, RFCG, Vol. 1, p. 617.
60. J. Davis, RFCG, Vol. 1, p. 680.
61. J. Davis, RFCG, Vol. 2, p. 454.
62. J. Davis, RFCG, Vol. 1, p. 102.
63. J. Davis, RFCG, Vol. 2, p. 621.
64. J. Davis, RFCG, Vol. 1, p. 620.
65. J. Davis, RFCG, Vol. 1, p. 571.
66. J. Davis, RFCG, Vol. 1, p. 114.
67. J. Davis, RFCG, Vol. 1, pp. 118-119.
68. J. Davis, RFCG, Vol. 1, p. 119.
69. J. Davis, RFCG, Vol. 1, p. 120.
70. J. Davis, RFCG, Vol. 1, p. 120.
71. J. Davis, RFCG, Vol. 1, p. 120.
72. J. Davis, RFCG, Vol. 1, pp. 132-133.
73. Gilmore, pp. 270-271.
74. J. Davis, RFCG, Vol. 1, p. 323.
75. J. Davis, RFCG, Vol. 1, pp. 504-505.
76. J. Davis, RFCG, Vol. 2, p. 191.
77. J. Davis, RFCG, Vol. 2, p. 279.
78. J. Davis, RFCG, Vol. 2, pp. 279-280.
79. V. Davis, Vol. 1, p. 434.
80. J. Davis, RFCG, Vol. 1, p. 68.
81. J. Davis, RFCG, Vol. 1, pp. 169, 170.
82. Rives, Vol. 22, Pt. 2, p. 1533.
83. J. Davis, RFCG, Vol. 1, pp. 172-173.
84. J. Davis, RFCG, Vol. 1, pp. 194, 195.
85. V. Davis, Vol. 1, pp. 433-434.
86. Rives, Vol. 22, Pt. 2, p. 1533.
87. J. Davis, RFCG, Vol. 1, p. 227.
88. J. Davis, SHCSA, p. 9.
89. J. Davis, RFCG, Vol. 2, pp. 581-582.
90. J. Davis, RFCG, Vol. 2, p. 582.
91. J. Davis, RFCG, Vol. 1, pp. 32-33.
92. J. Davis, RFCG, Vol. 1, pp. 262-263.
93. J. Davis, RFCG, Vol. 1, p. 48.
94. J. Davis, RFCG, Vol. 1, pp. 48-49.
95. J. Davis, RFCG, Vol. 1, p. 49.
96. J. Davis, RFCG, Vol. 1, p. 33.
97. J. Davis, RFCG, Vol. 1, p. 33.
98. J. Davis, RFCG, Vol. 1, p. 34.
99. J. Davis, RFCG, Vol. 1, p. 79.
100. J. Davis, RFCG, Vol. 1, p. 41.
101. J. Davis, RFCG, Vol. 1, pp. 52-53.
102. J. Davis, RFCG, Vol. 1, pp. 55-56.
103. J. Davis, RFCG, Vol. 1, p. 56.
104. J. Davis, RFCG, Vol. 1, pp. 56-57.
105. J. Davis, RFCG, Vol. 2, pp. 187-188.
106. J. Davis, RFCG, Vol. 1, p. 622.
107. Victor, CHSRWU, Vol. 1, pp. 409-410.
108. J. Davis, RFCG, Vol. 2, p. 172.
109. J. Davis, RFCG, Vol. 1, p. 322.

110. J. Davis, RFCG, Vol. 1, p. 76.
111. J. Davis, RFCG, Vol. 1, p. 243.
112. J. Davis, RFCG, Vol. 1, p. 250.
113. J. Davis, RFCG, Vol. 1, p. 250.
114. J. Davis, RFCG, Vol. 1, p. 298.
115. J. Davis, RFCG, Vol. 1, p. 68.
116. J. Davis, RFCG, Vol. 1, p. 85.
117. J. Davis, RFCG, Vol. 1, p. 177.
118. Victor, HCPMSR, Vol. 3, p. 38.
119. J. Davis, RFCG, Vol. 1, p. 168.
120. J. Davis, RFCG, Vol. 1, p. 618.
121. Gilmore, p. 268.
122. J. Davis, RFCG, Vol. 1, pp. 617-618.
123. J. Davis, RFCG, Vol. 1, p. 301.
124. J. Davis, RFCG, Vol. 1, p. 246.
125. J. Davis, RFCG, Vol. 1, p. 224.
126. J. Davis, RFCG, Vol. 1, p. 327.
127. J. Davis, RFCG, Vol. 1, pp. 184-185.
128. J. Davis, RFCG, Vol. 1, p. 223.
129. J. Davis, RFCG, Vol. 1, p. 185.
130. Alfriend, pp. 348-349.
131. J. Davis, RFCG, Vol. 1, p. 222.
132. J. Davis, RFCG, Vol. 1, p. 226.
133. J. Davis, RFCG, Vol. 1, pp. v-vi.
134. J. Davis, RFCG, Vol. 1, p. 231.
135. J. Davis, RFCG, Vol. 1, p. 297.
136. J. Davis, RFCG, Vol. 1, p. 314.
137. J. Davis, RFCG, Vol. 1, p. 324.
138. J. W. Jones, SHSP, p. 408.
139. J. W. Jones, SHSP, p. 408.
140. J. Davis, RFCG, Vol. 1, p. 306.
141. J. Davis, RFCG, Vol. 1, p. 485.
142. Moore, Vol. 1, p. 31.
143. Moore, Vol. 1, p. 31.
144. J. Davis, RFCG, Vol. 1, pp. 233-234.
145. J. Davis, RFCG, Vol. 1, p. 234.
146. Moore, Vol. 1, p. 31.
147. Moore, Vol. 1, p. 32.
148. J. Davis, RFCG, Vol. 1, p. 235.
149. J. Davis, RFCG, Vol. 1, p. 236.
150. J. Davis, RFCG, Vol. 1, p. 308.
151. J. Davis, RFCG, Vol. 1, p. 306.
152. Lowry and McCardle, p. 416 c.
153. J. Davis, RFCG, Vol. 1, p. 304. For more on the Confederate Constitution, see Seabrook, *The Constitution of the Confederate States of American Explained*, passim.
154. J. Davis, RFCG, Vol. 1, p. 259.
155. J. Davis, RFCG, Vol. 1, p. 259.
156. J. Davis, RFCG, Vol. 1, p. 260.
157. J. Davis, RFCG, Vol. 1, p. 260.
158. J. Davis, RFCG, Vol. 1, pp. 261-262.
159. J. Davis, RFCG, Vol. 1, p. 262.
160. J. Davis, RFCG, Vol. 1, p. 262.
161. McClellan, p. 296.
162. Moore, Vol. 4, p. 201.
163. J. Davis, RFCG, Vol. 1, pp. 506-507.
164. J. Davis, RFCG, Vol. 1, p. 263. The "popular Northern journal" quote is from the *New York Herald*, March 19, 1861.

165. Victor, CHSRWU, Vol. 1, p. 410.
166. J. Davis, RFCG, Vol. 1, p. 232.
167. J. Davis, RFCG, Vol. 1, pp. 205-206.
168. J. Davis, RFCG, Vol. 1, p. 206.
169. J. D. Richardson, Vol. 1, p. 569.
170. Smith, pp. 335-336.
171. J. Davis, RFCG, Vol. 1, p. 78.
172. J. Davis, RFCG, Vol. 2, p. 192.
173. J. Davis, RFCG, Vol. 1, p. viii.
174. J. Davis, SHCSA, p. 44.
175. J. Davis, SHCSA, p. 44.
176. V. Davis, Vol. 1, pp. 405-406.
177. Gilmore, p. 268.
178. Riley, p. 98.
179. Rives, Vol. 23, Pt. 1, p. 288.
180. J. Davis, RFCG, Vol. 1, p. 78.
181. J. Davis, RFCG, Vol. 1, pp. 3-4.
182. J. Davis, RFCG, Vol. 1, pp. 77-78.
183. J. Davis, RFCG, Vol. 1, pp. 4-5.
184. J. Davis, RFCG, Vol. 1, p. 303.
185. J. Davis, RFCG, Vol. 1, pp. 515, 516.
186. J. Davis, RFCG, Vol. 1, p. 534.
187. J. Davis, RFCG, Vol. 1, p. 622.
188. J. Davis, SHCSA, p. 37.
189. J. Davis, RFCG, Vol. 1, pp. 297-298.
190. J. Davis, RFCG, Vol. 1, p. 330.
191. J. Davis, RFCG, Vol. 1, pp. 335, 334.
192. J. Davis, RFCG, Vol. 2, pp. 179-180.
193. J. Davis, RFCG, Vol. 2, p. 182.
194. J. Davis, RFCG, Vol. 2, pp. 187-188.
195. J. Davis, RFCG, Vol. 2, p. 6.
196. J. Davis, RFCG, Vol. 2, p. 298.
197. J. Davis, RFCG, Vol. 2, pp. 621-622.
198. J. Davis, RFCG, Vol. 2, p. 170.
199. McClellan, p. 271.
200. J. W. Jones, SHSP, p. 408.
201. J. Davis, RFCG, Vol. 2, p. 683.
202. J. Davis, RFCG, Vol. 1, p. 300.
203. J. Davis, RFCG, Vol. 1, p. 321.
204. J. Davis, RFCG, Vol. 2, p. 4.
205. J. Davis, RFCG, Vol. 1, p. 292.
206. J. Davis, RFCG, Vol. 1, p. 251.
207. J. Davis, RFCG, Vol. 1, pp. 257-258.
208. J. Davis, RFCG, Vol. 1, p. vii.
209. J. Davis, RFCG, Vol. 1, p. 247.
210. J. Davis, RFCG, Vol. 2, p. 159.
211. J. Davis, RFCG, Vol. 2, pp. 159-160.
212. J. Davis, RFCG, Vol. 1, pp. 321, 320.
213. Moore, Vol. 1, p. 298.
214. J. A. Richardson, p. 509.
215. Moore, Vol. 1, p. 298.
216. J. Davis, RFCG, Vol. 2, pp. 160-161.
217. Gilmore, p. 271.
218. Gilmore, p. 272.
219. J. Davis, SHCSA, p. 500.
220. J. Davis, RFCG, Vol. 1, p. 439.
221. J. Davis, RFCG, Vol. 1, p. 249.

222. Gilmore, p. 262.
223. J. Davis, RFCG, Vol. 1, p. 204.
224. Gilmore, p. 263.
225. Gilmore, pp. 263-264.
226. J. Davis, RFCG, Vol. 2, pp. 563-564, 629.
227. J. Davis, RFCG, Vol. 2, pp. 656-657.
228. J. Davis, SHCSA, p. 501.
229. J. Davis, RFCG, Vol. 2, p. 570.
230. Gilmore, p. 265.
231. J. Davis, SHCSA, p. 30.
232. Gilmore, p. 266.
233. J. Davis, RFCG, Vol. 2, p. 13.
234. J. Davis, RFCG, Vol. 1, p. 310.
235. J. Davis, SHCSA, p. 83.
236. J. Davis, RFCG, Vol. 1, p. 181.
237. J. Davis, RFCG, Vol. 1, p. 518.
238. J. Davis, RFCG, Vol. 2, p. 2.
239. J. Davis, RFCG, Vol. 2, p. 2.
240. J. Davis, RFCG, Vol. 2, pp. 2-3.
241. J. Davis, RFCG, Vol. 2, p. 14.
242. J. Davis, RFCG, Vol. 2, p. 15.
243. J. Davis, RFCG, Vol. 2, p. 16.
244. J. Davis, RFCG, Vol. 2, pp. 307-308.
245. J. Davis, RFCG, Vol. 2, pp. 285-286.
246. J. Davis, RFCG, Vol. 2, pp. 287-289.
247. J. Davis, RFCG, Vol. 2, p. 289.
248. J. Davis, RFCG, Vol. 2, pp. 588-589.
249. J. Davis, RFCG, Vol. 2, p. 468.
250. J. Davis, RFCG, Vol. 2, p. 478.
251. J. Davis, RFCG, Vol. 2, pp. 502-503.
252. J. Davis, RFCG, Vol. 2, p. 503.
253. Victor, HCPMSR, Vol. 3, p. 40.
254. J. Davis, RFCG, Vol. 2, p. 594.
255. J. Davis, RFCG, Vol. 2, p. 606.
256. Victor, HCPMSR, Vol. 3, p. 38.
257. J. Davis, RFCG, Vol. 2, p. 607.
258. J. Davis, RFCG, Vol. 1, p. 440.
259. Addey, p. 112.
260. J. Davis, RFCG, Vol. 2, p. 160.
261. J. Davis, RFCG, Vol. 1, p. 443.
262. Moore, Vol. 1, p. 297.
263. Moore, Vol. 1, p. 297.
264. J. Davis, RFCG, Vol. 2, p. 22.
265. J. D. Richardson, Vol. 1, p. 568.
266. J. Davis, RFCG, Vol. 1, p. 313.
267. J. D. Richardson, Vol. 1, p. 569.
268. J. Davis, RFCG, Vol. 2, p. 191.
269. Victor, CHSRWU, Vol. 1, p. 409.
270. J. Davis, RFCG, Vol. 2, p. 183.
271. Moore, Vol. 1, p. 295.
272. J. Davis, RFCG, Vol. 2, pp. 5-6.
273. Moore, Vol. 1, p. 295.
274. Moore, Vol. 3, p. 406.
275. J. Davis, RFCG, Vol. 2, p. 4.
276. J. Davis, RFCG, Vol. 2, pp. 697, 696.
277. J. Davis, RFCG, Vol. 2, p. 705.
278. J. Davis, RFCG, Vol. 2, pp. 718-719.

279. J. Davis, RFCG, Vol. 2, pp. 721-722.
280. J. Davis, RFCG, Vol. 1, p. vii.
281. J. Davis, SHCSA, p. 504.
282. J. Davis, SHCSA, p. 503.
283. J. Davis, SHCSA, pp. 504-505.
284. Pollard, LC, p. 749.
285. J. Davis, RFCG, Vol. 1, pp. 228-229.
286. J. Davis, RFCG, Vol. 1, p. viii.
287. J. Davis, RFCG, Vol. 2, pp. 294-295.
288. J. Davis, RFCG, Vol. 2, p. 294.
289. J. Davis, RFCG, Vol. 2, p. 294.
290. Lowry and McCardle, p. 416 b.
291. J. Davis, RFCG, Vol. 2, pp. 759-760.
292. J. Davis, RFCG, Vol. 2, pp. 734.
293. J. Davis, RFCG, Vol. 2, pp. 733-734.
294. J. Davis, RFCG, Vol. 2, p. 762.
295. J. Davis, RFCG, Vol. 2, p. 762.
296. J. Davis, RFCG, Vol. 2, p. 762.
297. J. Davis, RFCG, Vol. 2, p. 763.
298. Galloway, p. 34.
299. Galloway, p. 34.
300. Hill, p. 410.
301. Adams, p. 49.
302. J. W. Jones, DMV, p. 466.
303. J. W. Jones, DMV, p. 467.
304. J. W. Jones, DMV, pp. 467-468.
305. Russell, p. xv.
306. Daniel, p. 9.
307. J. W. Jones, DMV, p. 599.
308. J. W. Jones, DMV, p. 605.
309. J. W. Jones, DMV, p. 608.
310. J. Davis, RFCG, Vol. 1, pp. 157-158.

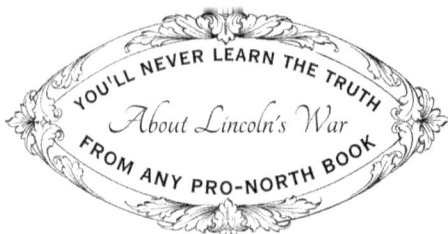

YOU'LL NEVER LEARN THE TRUTH
About Lincoln's War
FROM ANY PRO-NORTH BOOK

BIBLIOGRAPHY

Adams, Charles Francis. *Charles Francis Adams, 1835-1915: An Autobiography*. Boston, MA: Houghton Mifflin Co., 1916.

Addey, Markinfield. *Life and Imprisonment of Jefferson Davis*. New York, NY: M. Doolady, 1866.

Alfriend, Frank H. *The Life of Jefferson Davis*. Cincinnati, OH: Caxton Publishing House, 1868.

Daniel, John Warwick. *Oration by Hon. John W. Daniel on the Life, Services, and Character of Jefferson Davis* (delivered January 25, 1890). Richmond, VA: J. W. Randolph and Co., 1890.

Davis, Jefferson. *The Rise and Fall of the Confederate Government*. 2 vols. New York, NY: D. Appleton and Co., 1881.

——. *A Short History of the Confederates States of America*. New York, NY: Belford Co., 1890.

Davis, Varina (Howell). *Jefferson Davis: Ex-President of the Confederate States of America - A Memoir*. 2 vols. New York, NY: Belford Co., 1890.

Franklin, John Hope. *Reconstruction After the Civil War*. Chicago, IL: University of Chicago Press, 1961.

Galloway, Bishop Charles B. *Jefferson Davis: A Judicial Estimate*. Bulletin of the University of Mississippi, Ser. 6, August 1908 (address delivered June 3, 1908). Oxford, MS: University of Mississippi, 1908.

Gilmore, James Roberts. *Personal Recollections of Abraham Lincoln and the Civil War*. London, UK: John McQueen, 1899.

Hill, Benjamin H., Jr. *Senator Benjamin H. Hill of Georgia: His Life, Speeches, and Writings*. Atlanta, GA: T. H. P. Bloodworth, 1893.

Jones, John William. *Southern Historical Society Papers* (Vol. 14, January to December 1886). Richmond, VA: Southern Historical Society, 1886.

——. *The Davis Memorial Volume; or Our Dead President and the World's Tribute to His Memory*. Richmond, VA: B. F. Johnson, 1889.

Lowry, Robert, and William H. McCardle. *A History of Mississippi*. Jackson, MS: R. H. Henry and Co., 1891.

McCarty, Burke (ed.). *Little Sermons In Socialism by Abraham Lincoln*. Chicago, IL: The Chicago Daily Socialist, 1910.

McClellan, Rolander Guy. *Republicanism in the United States*. Philadelphia, PA: J. M. Stoddart and Co., 1872.

Moore, Frank (ed.). *The Rebellion Record: A Diary of American Events, With Documents, Narratives, Illustrative Incidents, Poetry, Etc.* 12 vols. New York, NY: G. P. Putnam, 1861.

Nicolay, John George, and John Hay (eds.). *Abraham Lincoln: Complete Works*. 12 vols. New York, NY: The Century Co., 1907.

Pollard, Edward Alfred. *The Lost Cause*. New York, NY: E. B. Treat and Co., 1867.

Richardson, James Daniel. *A Compilation of the Messages and Papers of the Confederacy*. 2 vols. Nashville, TN: United States Publishing Co., 1905.

Richardson, John Anderson. *Richardson's Defense of the South*. Atlanta, GA: A. B. Caldwell, 1914.

Riley, Franklin L. (ed.). *Publications of the Mississippi Historical Society* (Vol. 14). University, MS: Mississippi Historical Society, 1914.

Rives, John C. *Appendix to the Congressional Globe for the First Session, Thirty-First Congress: Containing Speeches and Important State Papers* (Vol. 22, Part 2). Washington, D.C.: John C. Rives, 1850.

——. *Appendix to the Congressional Globe for the First Session, Thirty-First Congress: Containing Speeches and Important State Papers* (Vol. 23, Part 1). Washington, D.C.: John C. Rives, 1850.

Russell, Charles Wells (ed.). *The Memoirs of John Singleton Mosby*. Boston, MA: Little, Brown, and Co., 1917.

Seabrook, Lochlainn. *Abraham Lincoln: The Southern View*. 2007. Franklin, TN: Sea Raven Press, 2010 ed.

——. *Everything You Were Taught About the Civil War is Wrong, Ask a Southerner!* Franklin, TN: Sea Raven Press, 2010.

——. *A Rebel Born: A Defense of Nathan Bedford Forrest*. Franklin, TN: Sea Raven Press, 2010.

——. *Everything You Were Taught About American Slavery is Wrong, Ask a Southerner!* Spring Hill, TN: Sea Raven Press, 2014.

——. *Confederacy 101: Amazing Facts You Never Knew About America's Oldest Political Tradition*. Spring Hill, TN: Sea Raven Press, 2015.

——. *Confederate Flag Facts: What Every American Should Know About Dixie's Southern Cross*. Spring Hill, TN: Sea Raven Press, 2015.

——. *Lincoln's War: The Real Cause, the Real Winner, the Real Loser*. Spring Hill, TN: Sea Raven Press, 2016.

——. *Abraham Lincoln Was a Liberal, Jefferson Davis Was a Conservative: The Missing Key to Understanding the American Civil War*. Spring Hill, TN: Sea Raven Press, 2017.

Smith, Alfred Emanuel (ed.). *The Outlook: A Weekly Newspaper* (Vol. 89, May-August 1908). New York, NY: The Outlook Co., 1908.

Victor, Orville James. *The History, Civil, Political, and Military, of the Southern Rebellion, From its Incipient Stages to its Close* (Vol. 3). New York, NY: James D. Torrey, 1861.

——. *The Comprehensive History of the Southern Rebellion and the War for the Union* (Vol. 1.) New York, NY: James D. Torrey, 1862.

MEET THE AUTHOR

LOCHLAINN SEABROOK, a neo-Victorian, is a well respected man of letters, a Kentucky Colonel, and the winner of the prestigious Jefferson Davis Historical Gold Medal for his "masterpiece," *A Rebel Born: A Defense of Nathan Bedford Forrest.* A classic littérateur and an unreconstructed Southern historian, he is an award-winning author, Civil War scholar, Bible authority, and a traditional Southern Agrarian of Scottish, English, Irish, Dutch, Welsh, German, and Italian extraction.

A child prodigy, Seabrook is today a true Renaissance Man whose occupational titles also include encyclopedist, lexicographer, musician, artist, graphic designer, genealogist, photographer, and award-winning poet. Also a songwriter and a screenwriter, he has a 40 year background in historical nonfiction writing and is a member of the Sons of Confederate Veterans, the Civil War Trust, and the National Grange.

Due to similarities in their writing styles, ideas, and literary works, Seabrook is often referred to as the "new Shelby Foote," the "Southern Joseph Campbell," and the "American Robert Graves" (his English cousin). Seabrook coined the terms "South-shaming" and "Lincolnian liberalism," and holds the world's record for writing the most books on Nathan Bedford Forrest: nine. In addition, Seabrook is the first Civil War scholar to connect the early American nickname for the U.S., "The Confederate States of America," with the Southern Confederacy that arose eight decades later, and the first to note that in 1860 the party platforms of the two major political parties were the opposite of what they are today (Victorian Democrats were conservatives, Victorian Republicans were liberals).

Above, Colonel Lochlainn Seabrook, award-winning Civil War scholar and unreconstructed Southern historian. America's most popular and prolific pro-South author, his many books have introduced hundreds of thousands to the truth about the War for Southern Independence. He coined the phrase "South-shaming" and holds the world's record for writing the most books on Nathan Bedford Forrest: nine.

The grandson of an Appalachian coal-mining family, Seabrook is a seventh-generation Kentuckian, co-chair of the Jent/Gent Family Committee (Kentucky), founder and director of the Blakeney Family Tree Project, and a board member of the Friends of Colonel Benjamin E. Caudill. Seabrook's literary works have been endorsed by leading authorities, museum curators, award-winning historians, bestselling authors, celebrities, noted scientists, well respected educators, TV show hosts and producers, renowned military artists, esteemed Southern organizations, and distinguished academicians from around the world.

Seabrook has authored over 50 popular adult books on the American Civil War, American and international slavery, the U.S. Confederacy (1781), the Southern Confederacy (1861), religion, theology and thealogy, Jesus, the Bible, the Apocrypha, the Law of Attraction, alternative health, spirituality, ghost stories, the paranormal, ufology, social issues, and cross-cultural studies of the family and marriage. His Confederate biographies, pro-South studies, genealogical monographs, family histories, military encyclopedias, self-help guides, and etymological dictionaries have received wide acclaim.

Seabrook's eight children's books include a Southern guide to the Civil War, a biography of Nathan Bedford Forrest, a dictionary of religion and myth, a rewriting of the King Arthur legend (which reinstates the original pre-Christian motifs), two bedtime stories for preschoolers, a naturalist's guidebook to owls, a worldwide look at the family, and an examination of the Near-Death Experience.

Of blue-blooded Southern stock through his Kentucky, Tennessee, Virginia, West Virginia, and North Carolina ancestors, he is a direct descendant of European royalty via his 6th great-grandfather, the Earl of Oxford, after which London's famous Harley Street is named. Among his celebrated male Celtic ancestors is Robert the Bruce, King of Scotland, Seabrook's 22nd great-grandfather. The 21st great-grandson of Edward I "Longshanks" Plantagenet), King of England, Seabrook is a thirteenth-generation Southerner through his descent from the colonists of Jamestown, Virginia (1607).

The 2nd, 3rd, and 4th great-grandson of dozens of Confederate soldiers, one of his closest connections to Lincoln's War is through his 3rd great-grandfather, Elias Jent, Sr., who fought for the Confederacy in the Thirteenth Cavalry Kentucky under Seabrook's 2nd cousin, Colonel Benjamin E. Caudill. The Thirteenth, also known as "Caudill's Army," fought in numerous conflicts, including the Battles of Saltville, Gladsville, Mill Cliff, Poor Fork, Whitesburg, and Leatherwood.

Seabrook is a direct descendant of the families of Alexander H. Stephens, John Singleton Mosby, William Giles Harding, and Edmund Winchester Rucker, and is related to the following Confederates and other 18th- and 19th-Century luminaries: Robert E. Lee, Stephen Dill Lee, Stonewall Jackson, Nathan Bedford Forrest, James Longstreet, John Hunt Morgan, Jeb Stuart, Pierre G. T. Beauregard (approved the Confederate Battle Flag design), George W. Gordon, John Bell Hood, Alexander Peter Stewart, Arthur M. Manigault, Joseph Manigault, Charles Scott Venable, Thornton A. Washington, John A. Washington, Abraham Buford, Edmund W. Pettus, Theodrick "Tod" Carter, John B. Womack, John H. Winder, Gideon J. Pillow, States Rights Gist, Henry R. Jackson, John Lawton Seabrook, John C. Breckinridge, Leonidas Polk, Zachary Taylor, Sarah Knox Taylor (first wife of Jefferson Davis), Richard Taylor, Davy Crockett, Daniel Boone, Meriwether Lewis (of the Lewis and Clark Expedition) Andrew Jackson, James K. Polk, Abram Poindexter Maury (founder of Franklin, TN), Zebulon Vance, Thomas Jefferson, Edmund Jennings Randolph, George Wythe Randolph (grandson of Jefferson), Felix K. Zollicoffer, Fitzhugh Lee, Nathaniel F. Cheairs, Jesse James, Frank James, Robert Brank Vance, Charles Sidney Winder, John W. McGavock, Caroline E. (Winder) McGavock, David Harding McGavock, Lysander

McGavock, James Randal McGavock, Randal William McGavock, Francis McGavock, Emily McGavock, William Henry F. Lee, Lucius E. Polk, Minor Meriwether (husband of noted pro-South author Elizabeth Avery Meriwether), Ellen Bourne Tynes (wife of Forrest's chief of artillery, Captain John W. Morton), South Carolina Senators Preston Smith Brooks and Andrew Pickens Butler, and famed South Carolina diarist Mary Chesnut.

Seabrook's modern day cousins include: Patrick J. Buchanan (conservative author), Cindy Crawford (model), Shelby Lee Adams (Letcher Co., Kentucky, photographer), Bertram Thomas Combs (Kentucky's 50th governor), Edith Bolling (wife of President Woodrow Wilson), and actors Andy Griffith, George C. Scott, Robert Duvall, Reese Witherspoon, Lee Marvin, Rebecca Gayheart, and Tom Cruise.

Seabrook's screenplay, *A Rebel Born*, based on his book of the same name, has been signed with acclaimed filmmaker Christopher Forbes (of Forbes Film). It is now in pre-production, and is set for release in 2017 as a full-length feature film. This will be the first movie ever made of Nathan Bedford Forrest's life story, and as a historically accurate project written from the Southern perspective, is destined to be one of the most talked about Civil War films of all time.

Born with music in his blood, Seabrook is an award-winning, multi-genre, BMI-Nashville songwriter and lyricist who has composed some 3,000 songs (250 albums), and whose original music has been heard in film (*A Rebel Born, Cowgirls 'n Angels, Confederate Cavalry, Billy the Kid: Showdown in Lincoln County, Vengeance Without Mercy, Last Step, County Line, The Mark*) and on TV and radio worldwide. A musician, producer, multi-instrumentalist, and renown performer—whose keyboard work has been variously compared to pianists from Hargus Robbins and Vince Guaraldi to Elton John and Leonard Bernstein—Seabrook has opened for groups

The author's cousins, General Stonewall Jackson (left) and General Robert E. Lee (center), meet with President Davis prior to the Battle of Seven Days in the summer of 1862.

such as the Earl Scruggs Review, Ted Nugent, and Bob Seger, and has performed privately for such public figures as President Ronald Reagan, Burt Reynolds, Loni Anderson, and Senator Edward W. Brooke. Seabrook's cousins in the music business include: Johnny Cash, Elvis Presley, Billy Ray and Miley Cyrus, Patty Loveless, Tim McGraw, Lee Ann Womack, Dolly Parton, Pat Boone, Naomi, Wynonna, and Ashley Judd, Ricky Skaggs, the Sunshine Sisters, Martha Carson, and Chet Atkins.

Seabrook lives with his wife and family in historic Middle Tennessee, the heart of Forrest country and the Confederacy, where his conservative Southern ancestors fought valiantly against Liberal Lincoln and the progressive North in defense of Jeffersonianism, constitutional government, and personal liberty.

LochlainnSeabrook.com

MEET THE FOREWORD WRITER

PERCIVAL BEACROFT is a native Texan and a graduate of Southern Methodist University with degrees in History and Law. Graduate International Law studies were at University of London and later employment in the field of Literary and Theatrical representation in New York.

His interest in Jefferson Davis and Constitutional Law began as a teenager and this interest has continued his entire life. In 1971 he purchased the neglected plantation house of Davis' parents, Rosemont Plantation, near Woodville, Mississippi, and restored the home, which had been built by them in 1810. After restoration it was developed as a museum which portrays the lives of Jefferson Davis' family from 1810 until it was sold by them in 1895. Davis' mother and others of his family are buried in the family cemetery at Rosemont and it is open to the public.

In 1973 Beacroft was a founder of the Davis Family Association, which has met at Rosemont every two years until the present time. The members are descendants of Jefferson Davis as well as those of his siblings. The family cemetery is on the grounds of Rosemont. The only Davis family genealogy has been done at Rosemont by Ernesto Caldeira and published in the Papers of Jefferson Davis. It is an ongoing project with over 3,000 descendants and their statistics.

He has been a Trustee of the Papers of Jefferson Davis since 1973, which is a monumental work of 14 volumes consisting of the extant letters to and from Davis, which have been edited at Rice University, Houston, Texas and printed by LSU Press in Baton Rouge, Louisiana. Numerous historical literary awards were given to this publication.

Beacroft has also developed, funded, and produced the only documentary film of the entire life of Jefferson Davis. It is an award winning mini-series in three episodes and has been shown on many PBS Stations across the country. It is entitled *Jefferson Davis, an American President*.

He is of Confederate ancestry and is a member of the Military Order of Stars and Bars, The Sons of Confederate Veterans, and Sons of the American Revolution.

Keep Your Body, Mind, & Spirit Vibrating at Their Highest Level

YOU CAN DO SO BY READING THE BOOKS OF

SEA RAVEN PRESS

There is nothing that will so perfectly keep your body, mind, and spirit in a healthy condition as to think wisely and positively. Hence you should not only read this book, but also the other books that we offer. They will quicken your physical, mental, and spiritual vibrations, enabling you to maintain a position in society as a healthy erudite person.

KEEP YOURSELF WELL-INFORMED!

The well-informed person is always at the head of the procession, while the ignorant, the lazy, and the unthoughtful hang onto the rear. If you are a Spiritual man or woman, do yourself a great favor: read Sea Raven Press books and stay well posted on the Truth. It is almost criminal for one to remain in ignorance while the opportunity to gain knowledge is open to all at a nominal price.

We invite you to visit our Webstore for a wide selection of wholesome, family-friendly, well-researched, educational books for all ages. You will be glad you did!

Five-Star Books & Gifts From the Heart of the American South

SeaRavenPress.com

Some Final Words From President Davis

"The position of the South was justified by the Constitution. . . . In the forum of conscience, the Confederacy stands fully acquitted. . . . [Thus] never question or teach your children to desecrate the memory of the [Confederate] dead . . . that their brothers were wrong in the effort to maintain the sovereignty, freedom and independence which was their inalienable birthright."

If you enjoyed this book you will be interested in Colonel Seabrook's other popular related titles:

☛ EVERYTHING YOU WERE TAUGHT ABOUT THE CIVIL WAR IS WRONG, ASK A SOUTHERNER!
☛ EVERYTHING YOU WERE TAUGHT ABOUT AMERICAN SLAVERY IS WRONG, ASK A SOUTHERNER!
☛ CONFEDERATE FLAG FACTS: WHAT EVERY AMERICAN SHOULD KNOW ABOUT DIXIE'S SOUTHERN CROSS
☛ CONFEDERACY 101: AMAZING FACTS YOU NEVER KNEW ABOUT AMERICA'S OLDEST POLITICAL TRADITION

Available from Sea Raven Press and wherever fine books are sold

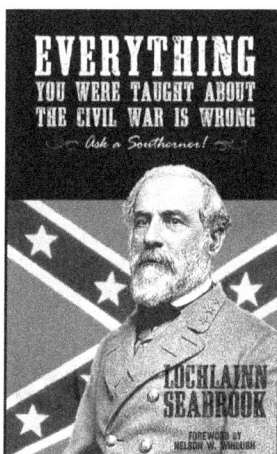

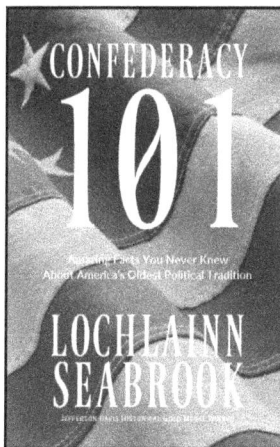

ALL OF OUR BOOK COVERS ARE AVAILABLE AS 11" X 17" POSTERS, SUITABLE FOR FRAMING.

SeaRavenPress.com • NathanBedfordForrestBooks.com

9 7 8 0 9 8 3 8 1 8 5 1 9